Programming

3 Manuscripts in 1 Book

JOSEPH MINING

The reproduction, transmission, and duplication of any of the content found

herein, including any specific or extended information will be done as an illegal act regardless of the end form the information ultimately takes. This includes copied versions of the work both physical, digital and audio unless express consent of the Publisher is provided beforehand.

The only exception is for the inclusion of brief quotations in a review. Any additional rights reserved.

Furthermore, the information that can be found within the pages described

forthwith shall be considered both accurate and truthful when it comes to the

recounting of facts. As such, any use, correct or incorrect, of the provided

information will render the Publisher free of responsibility as to the actions taken

outside of their direct purview. Regardless, there are zero scenarios where the

original author or the Publisher can be deemed liable in any fashion for any

damages or hardships that may result from any of the information discussed herein.

Additionally, the information in the following pages is intended only for
informational purposes and should thus be thought of as universal. As befitting its nature, it is presented without assurance regarding its prolonged validity or interim quality. Trademarks that are mentioned are done without written consent and can in no way be considered an endorsement from the trademark holder.

Table of Contents

Machine Learning

A Comprehensive Journey From Beginner To Advanced Level To Understand WHY You MUST Keep Pace With Innovation, Artificial Intelligence And Big Data With Practical Examples

JOSEPH MINING

Introduction

The following chapters will discuss everything you need to know to get started with machine learning. The world of technology is growing at a fast pace. There seem to be new things coming out on the market all the time, and the consumer is ready to welcome it in and enjoy every minute of the whole thing. But due to this increase in demand, programmers need to find newer and better ways to impress the customer, and machine learning is helping them to do that.

While different components come with machine learning, it is important to realize that this is a way of coding that allows the computer or the other pieces of technology to learn as it goes. The user can put in any input they would like (without the programmer trying to figure it all out ahead of time and make guesses), and the computer will use past experiences and other information to help out and learn over time. It is a neat thing that has shaped a lot of the technology industry, including spam filtering, search engines, voice recognition, and more.

This guidebook will talk more about machine learning and all of the different parts that come with it. Inside, we will start with some of the basics of machine learning. We will look at what machine learning is, why it is so beneficial to learn, and even how it compares to artificial intelligence and more.

From there, we are going to take a look at how we can add statistics and probability into this mix to help make machine learning more effective overall, and some of the building blocks needed to help with machine learning. Through all of this, we will look at examples and formulas that help to bring this alive and ensures that you are going to understand how these affect machine learning fully.

To end this guidebook, we will take a look at some of the basic algorithms found with machine learning. These include the three basic machine learning, including supervised learning, unsupervised learning, and reinforcement learning. Inside each, we will talk about the algorithms, the strengths, and weaknesses of each, and when you would benefit from using them all.

Machine learning is changing the way technology works, and there are a ton of opportunities that come with it. There are so many possibilities that are now available to us; thanks to machine learning that wasn't possible with some of the traditional coding methods that we have used in the past. When you are ready to learn more about how machine learning works and how you can utilize it on some of your projects, make sure to check out this guidebook to help you get started!

There are plenty of books on this subject on the market, thanks again for choosing this one! Every effort was made to ensure it is full of as much useful information as possible. Please enjoy!

Chapter 1: What is Machine Learning?

If you have spent any time looking up information about technology and where our world is going now in terms of using computers and programming, then you have likely spent at least a little time hearing about machine learning. Whether you were intrigued by this term or only saw it pop up on some of the articles you were reading, you will find that working with machine learning is a crucial thing to know. It can open the doors to new programming that you can do, and can make life easier when developing the software and technology that you want.

If you are new to this arena and haven't spent much time with programming, then it is possible you have never even heard about machine learning. Even so, it is likely that at one point or another, you have used machine learning to help make your life easier. For example, if you have ever done a query on a search engine, such as on Google, then it was the technology of machine learning that made this possible. The machine learning is the program that runs these search engine sites and helps you find the results that you.

Machine learning technology is the only way you will be able to get these programs to work. Regular coding is not able to do this complex task. The system needs to read through your request, look through millions of websites, and then pick out the one that matches up to your needs. And in the beginning, it may not do the best job picking out what you want. But thanks to the machine learning technology behind it, these programs can learn your search preferences and will learn exactly what you are looking for based on your choice.

That is one of the many examples that can come with how we will use machine learning to do some amazing things. Not only can the use of search engines benefit from this technology, but you can use it in many other applications, such as trying to figure out whether to consider message spam or not.

Unlike some of the conventional programming methods that you may have used in the past, machine learning can help programs not just to sit still and give out predetermined outputs. This works in some cases, but it is not going to be efficient for a lot of the things we want to do. Unlike these conventional programs, machine learning programs are designed to learn and adapt based on the behavior that the user portrays to it. This is excellent because it ensures that the user is going to get the results that they want, rather than being frustrated along the way.

If a computer or another form of technology already has some machine learning capabilities or programs on it, then it can be programmed in a way to form the inputs that the user gives to it. This means that the computer can provide the user with the results, or the answers, that are needed, even if the problem is more complicated. The input for this learning process, which is often known as a learning algorithm will be known as data training in this process.

Understanding machine learning

When we are talking about machine learning, it is the process of teaching the program or the computer to use some of its experiences that happen over time, the experiences with the user to do a better job in providing results in the future.

An excellent example of this would be a program that used to filter out the spam emails that you get. There are a few different methods out there that you can use to make this happen. But one of the easiest ones is to teach the computer how you would like it to identify, memorize, and categorize all the emails in your inbox by labeling them as either safe or spam when they first enter into your email.

As you do this over time, the computer will learn which emails you think are spam, and which ones are more important to you. Then, if there is a new email that does come in at a later tie, the program is going to take a look at how you treated similar emails in the past and will take care of them in this matter. Over time, the program is going to be great at marking the right emails spam and leaving the others alone, but there is often a few trial and errors that happen along the way.

While this is a proper technique of memorization to work with when you want to teach the program how to do these processes, there are going to be some things that are going to fall short with it. First, this method is going to miss out on a little thing known as inductive reasoning. This is something that has to be there, even with a program using machine learning, so that the computer can learn efficiently.

As a programmer, you may find that it is better you go through and do some programming on the computer, this way, you can teach it how to discern the message types (or do the other tasks that you want with this process). Rather than trying to ask the computer to go through the process and the effort it takes to memorize all of that information.

To make sure this is a process that is as simple as possible, you would need to do some programming of the computer. This programming would involve the computer scanning any email that is in your spam folder, or anything that it already knows as spam. From this scan, the program can recognize some of the keywords and phrases that tend to show up in these messages.

With this information in place, the computer can scan through any of the new emails that try to get into your inbox. And if there is one that matches up with a lot of key phrases and words, then they will be sent to the spam folder without you even knowing.

This method may sound like it takes a lot more time to accomplish than some of the others, and you may wonder why you would want to work with this method compared to doing the other one. But it is one of the best, though there are a few things to watch. You have to be actively involved in this machine learning and have the realization that sometimes, the program is going to do things in a wrong way, or some spam messages will get through to your inbox, and some that aren't spam will end up in your spam folder.

While a person would be able to read through these emails and see the issue right away, the computer is learning as it goes. And it is much faster at doing this process. It can look through hundreds of emails in a few seconds and usually sort them correctly. But when it comes to humans, this would not happen. You would have more accuracy, but your speed would be quite a bit lower.

So, machine learning is going to be a process where you will teach the computer how to learn. The program will be able to use some of the information that it already has, along with the past interactions with the user that it has, and then learn the appropriate response to help it react in the manner that you would like. There are a lot of different applications that can use this, including search engines, voice recognition, and spam email filtering. And as the world of technology grows and changes, even more, more and more applications of this kind of technology will likely end up coming out as well.

What are the benefits of working with machine learning?

At this point, you may be wondering why you would want to learn how to work with machine learning. There are many different things that machine learning can help you with, but there are two main ones that we are going to focus on right now.

The first one includes that using machine learning means you are going to be able to handle any task that is too complex for the programmer to place into the computer. The second is going to include that machine learning can help with adaptively generated tasks that need to be done.

With that in mind, let's look at a few situations, and why you would have to use machines to ensure they are going to work with your program.

Complicated tasks

One way that you can use machine learning is to help with some complicated programming tasks. There will be some tasks that you can work on in programming that may not respond that well to conventional programming. These tasks may not have the right amount of clarity that you need to use a conventional program, or they have too much complexity with them.

The first set would be tasks that people and animals can perform. Think about speech recognition, image recognition, and driving as examples. Humans can do these, but if you used conventional programming tools to teach the computer how to do this, it is going to run into trouble. It is much better for the computer to learn the right way to do these tasks by receiving good outputs when they are right. Machine learning can help make this happen.

The second benefit is that machine learning can help with tasks that are too hard for humans to do. These would include things such as going through a complex analysis where there is too much data for one person to go through. Companies may decide to use machine learning when they wish to go through a ton of data and make decisions and predictions.

Also, machine learning can be used similarly to help with genomic data, search engines, and weather prediction. There is going to be some valuable information in all of the data sets, but humans may not have the energy or the time to go through this information, at least not promptly so they will use machine learning to do it for them.

While traditional forms of programming can do a lot of amazing things and have worked for years to help programmers get things done, some tasks don't work that well with these. Machine learning can fill in the gaps and get you the expected results.

Adaptively generated tasks

If you have worked with programming in the past, you were likely able to get these programs to do a lot of amazing things along the way. Even though these can do a lot of great things to help you grow your knowledge of machine learning, there are some limitations to what that programming can do.

One of these limitations is that the programming methods are going to be rigid. This means that once you are done writing out the code, and you turn it on to implement it, the codes will always be the same. These codes are going to do the same things over and over again, that is, unless you specifically go in and change up some of the code. But these codes will never be able to learn and adapt on their own.

There will be some times when you would like to create a new program, and you want it to be able to act out in different manners, or you will want it to give a reaction that goes with the input it is receiving. This is something that a conventional programming language is not going to be able to do. This is where machine learning is going to come in because it allows you to write out codes so that the program can learn and make changes.

Machine learning is easy to work with

We shall talk about a few different algorithms and tasks that work with machine learning in a bit. And as you look through these, they will seem like they are a bit complicated. But they are pretty simple, and it shows you all of the cool things you can do when you utilize machine learning. Many of these tasks are going to be useful, but they are too complicated to do with conventional programming methods. This would include things like facial recognition and speech recognition. While traditional forms of programming would have trouble with these, machine learning can handle them with ease.

Machine learning is a great thing to learn because you can teach a program and technology on how to learn as it goes along. An excellent example is speech recognition. This thing is going to use machine learning to figure out what you are saying and what you need. In the beginning, the program is going to struggle a bit, trying to learn your accent and the words you use frequently. For the first little bit, it is possible you will need to repeat words and phrases to help the program understand what you are saying.

Over time though, as you use the program, the speech recognition is going to get much better at the job that it is doing, and it will get the answer right the first time. The program will learn your speech patterns, your accent, and some of the other things that it needs to get the answer right. Sometimes, if you use the program long enough, it is going to become good at making predictions for you and can provide you with the answers to these predictions as well.

If machine learning is put to use properly, it can do this learning process, regardless of the device that it is on. This means that it will learn to listen to the way each person speaks on that device. This is hard to do with traditional programming options that you may have used in the past, and even if you could do it with these, the code would be complicated. But, as we progress through this guidebook, you will be able to use some simple machine learning codes to get similar results in no time.

While you can bring out machine learning to complete several complex actions, it is sometimes easier to use the codes that come with machine learning than you would assume. If you have ever been able to code and use programming languages of any kind in the past, you will find that working with machine learning doesn't have to be as complicated as it seems, and you will already have the basics understanding from this past knowledge.

Another thing you will like about machine learning is that there are a few different options that you can use, depending on the program you would like to work with. The three main types, which we are going to explore a bit more as this guidebook progresses, are going to include unsupervised learning, reinforcement learning, and supervised learning. When you start to use the different methods provided in this guidebook to handle these learning, it becomes so much easier to get the code and the program to react the way that you would like.

As you can see, there are a lot of benefits that come with machine learning, and you will be able to use them all to help you do a lot of cool programming tasks. We will be able to see some of the different applications of machine learning in the later part of this book, but you will notice that this opens up a lot of doors to you in terms of what you can do with coding and programming.

How can I use machine learning?

As you start looking at machine learning, you may notice that it has changed a lot over the years, and the different things that programmers are now able to do with it are pretty unique and fun. There are many established firms, as well as startups, that are using machine learning because it has done some fantastic things to help their business grow. While there are a lot of applications that machine learning can help you out with, some of the best methods include:

- Statistical research: machine learning is a big part of IT now. You will find out that machine learning will help you to go through a lot of complexity when looking through large data patterns. Some of the options using statistical research include search engines, credit cards, and filtering spam messages.

- Big data analysis: many companies need to be able to get through a lot of data in a short time. They use this data to recognize how their customers spend money, and even to make decisions and predictions. This used to take a long time to have someone sit through and look at the data, but now, machine learning can do the process faster and much more efficiently. Options like election campaigns, medical fields, and retail stores have used machine learning for this purpose.

- Finances: some finance companies have also used machine learning. Stock trading online has seen a rise in the use of machine learning to help make efficient and safe decisions, and so much more.

As mentioned, these are only a few of the ways you could use machine learning to help your business. As you add it to your business with some IT, you will find that even more options are going to become available.

Are there different things machine learning can help with?

When you first hear about machine learning, you may assume that you are going to run into trouble finding ways to use this technology and coding to see the results that you want. You may think that there are only a few ways that this works and that the average programmer would not be able to utilize these techniques and see the results that they would like.

The neat thing about machine learning though is that there are a lot of ways that machine learning can help make your codes better, and you may be surprised at how many different applications can use machine learning. There are always programmers and companies who are looking at machine learning deeply to figure out what else they can do with it. With that said, some of the different challenges that machine learning is good at helping out with include

Search engines

An excellent example that we have brought up a bit before is the idea that it can help out with search engines. A search engine is going to take the input from the user, mainly their search query, and they will learn from the results that you push on from the list they provide. The first few times you start using the search engine, you will find that you may have to go down the page a bit to find the result that you think is the most relevant.

But, as your search engine starts to learn more about the way you look things up and what you like in terms of results, it is going to get better. Over time, as you continue to do a lot more searches over and over again, you will find that your selections will get closer to the top of the page. This is because the search engine, using machine learning, was able to get better at guessing the results that you are the most interested in.

Collaborative filtering

This is a challenge that a lot of online retailers can run into because they will use it to help them get more profits through sales. Think about when you are on a site like Amazon.com. After you do a few searches, you will then get recommendations for other products that you may want to try out. Amazon.com uses machine learning to figure out what items you would be interested in, in the hopes of helping you to make another purchase.

Doing translations

There are many times when we will want to take the words that we have and change them to another language. Whether we are taking our native language and translating over to a different language, or taking a different language and translating back to our native language, a good translation tool can make a world of difference.

If you are working with some program that is responsible for translating different things, this means that you are directly working with machine learning. The program at hand is trying to look through a document or some words, and then it is trying to recognize and understand the words that are there. It isn't just about the words themselves on this, though; it is also about the context of the words, the syntax, and grammar. And then, if the original document has some mistakes in it, the program is going to have an even harder time learning as it goes.

This process of machine learning can be complicated because it needs to teach the program how to take one language and translate it over to another one. And many times, these translation services need to be able to do this with more than one type of language. For example, there isn't a program that goes from English to French. It would go from English to French or Chinese, or German, or Spanish and back again. And then it may be able to do other combinations, such as German to French or Spanish to Chinese. This adds to the level of complication.

Name identity recognition

This programming is where the computer will need to be able to look at names and such, and figure out their entities. It needs to be able to look at the places, actions, names, and out of any document that it comes across. This can be used in a situation where you have a program that needs to digest and then also comprehends a document that you submit to it.

Let's say that you are looking through your email service, whether it is Gmail or some other kind. It is possible you can use this to send things out to new customers and then gives you the ability to look through a new address as soon as it comes to your inbox. From that email, it would automatically take the information and place it into the address book. This helps you to keep that information in one place, save time, and ensures that you are not going to lose the information along the way.

Speech recognition

Another way you can use machine learning is through speech recognition. This can be a hard one to work with because we have to consider the different sounds that each voice has, how the genders sound to one another, the various dialects that each person can use, speech patterns and fluctuations, and even different languages. The way someone is going to say a word out loud is going to be completely different than the way someone else may decide to use or say it. And the program needs to be able to catch and learn how to recognize these different patterns.

An excellent example of a product that uses this is the Amazon Echo. On this program, machine learning is being used hardcore to make it successful. This kind of program, along with the machine learning capabilities, can slowly learn the speech patterns of those who use it and then can use that information to respond properly. Of course, there are going to be some issues when you first get the device, and it is likely going to give you the wrong result or not understand you. But as you use the device some more, and as machine learning programs get more advanced, this is going to become less of a problem.

Facial recognition

Machine learning is going to help you out with facial recognition as well. This is going to require the system to work on several layers to figure out if the person in the picture is someone that it knows. This type would rely on photos, as well as videos so that only the people who hold the right authorization would be able to use that system.

The system would look at these videos and photos and figure out who is allowed on the system. Through a series of learning processes, it would then tell who can get onto the system, and who is not allowed there. If this is not set up the right way, then you may end up with those who are authorized not getting in and those without the proper authorization being able to get in. Machine learning will provide you the tools needed to get this done.

Just from this list, you can already see that there are a lot of things that machine learning will be able to help you out with. These are some of the beginning options, the ones that have been used so far. But over time, as more people start to learn how to work with machine learning, and accept that this is a great way to get their program to learn and develop more than anything else, we are likely going to see more and more ways that this technology is going to grow.

Chapter 2: Is Artificial Intelligence the Same as Machine Learning?

The next topic here is the idea of artificial intelligence and whether it is seen as the same thing as machine learning. To someone who has started reading through this guidebook, it may seem like machine learning, and artificial intelligence are the same thing. You may assume that we are talking about the same thing, or that they are pretty much the same thing, but this is just not true. Some big differences can occur between machine learning and artificial intelligence and understanding the differences that show up between them, and how each one works is going to work can make a big difference in how you use them.

With machine learning, you will find that the process can work well when working with data science, and it can work in artificial intelligence as well. To start with, when we talk about the term of data science, it is a pretty broad thing to consider, and it will have a lot of different concepts included. But one of these concepts, to keep it simple, is machine learning. Other concepts, though, will include data mining, big data, and artificial intelligence. Data science is a filed that is growing since it is so new, and it won't take long before people find more and more uses for this topic.

Statistics is vital when it comes to data science, and it can also be used often in machine learning. You would be able to work with classical statistics, even at the higher levels, so that the data set is going to stay consistent throughout. But the way you use it will depend on what data you are using, and how complex the information gets.

It is essential to understand the difference between the categories of artificial intelligence and machine learning. There are some instances where they can be very similar, but there are some significant differences, which is why they are considered two different things. Let's take a look at each of these to ensure we understand how they both work in data science.

What is artificial intelligence?

To help you figure out more about what machine learning and what artificial intelligence are, and how they are different, we are going to look at AI or artificial intelligence is all about. AI is a term that was first talked about in the 1950s, thanks to John McCarthy. AI was first used to describe a method you can use for manufactured devices to learn how to copy the capabilities of humans in mental tasks.

The term is used in a bit differently in our modern world, but the basic ideas are still the same with it. When you try to implement a program that uses AI, you will enable a machine, such as a computer, to operate and think in the same manner as a human brain can. This is something that is going to benefit you because not only will the AI device be able to think like a human; it can do it in a manner that is more efficient than the human brain can do.

When you are first getting started with these ideas, you may think that AI and machine learning are going to be the same thing. But some differences come along. Some people who don't understand these two terms, and how these terms work may think that they are the same. But often, the way they are going to be used in the world of programming is what makes them so different and unique.

How is machine learning different?

Then there is machine learning. This option is going to be a bit newer than some of the other parts of data science, and it is just twenty years old. But even though machine learning has been around for this long, the last few years have helped to bring this area into the limelight, and computers are finally changing enough that you can use machine learning more and more.

When it comes to data science, machine learning is going to be the part that can specifically focus on having the program learn from any given data input, and get better at making good predictions as well. The more the program is used, and the more the user can work with it, the better it will get at doing all of this work. For example, when you want to use the machine learning capabilities in a search engine, the user would put in some term into the query. Then the search engine will provide you with some matching pages that you can choose from to find the information that you want.

When you first start using this option on the search engine, you will find that the query results are not going to be as accurate as you would like. You may have to search down to a lower result to find what you want, and it won't be at the top. But, the more you can do queries on the search engine, the better that engine is going to be at picking out the information that you want and providing you with better choices.

So, with this in mind, your first few times using that search engine, you may click on a result on the lower end of the page, or move to the next page instead. But after you use this for a few weeks or more, you will be able to find the result that you want right at the top of the page.

If you have used traditional programming in the past, you may find that these codes are not able to do something like this. Each person is going to go through and put in different searches to their queries, even when they are looking for the same things. Plus, every person who is doing these kinds of searches online will have a preference when it comes to what they would like to pick out on the search engine. This makes it hard for them to work on a traditional code, but it is something that machine learning can do, and it can do it successfully.

Of course, the example of a search engine is one of the things that are you can do in machine learning. There are a lot of complex problems that you can do with your computer, thanks to machine learning. Sometimes, you will be able to work on these problems with the human brain, but you will often find that if you want to get it done quickly, and more efficiently, then the human brain is not the best for doing this, machine learning is.

Let's look at an example of when this would happen, and that will come with data mining. This often includes a lot of data, and often, this amount is so much and keeps coming in, that it is hard for a single person to go through in a timely or efficiently. And if there is more than one person who comes in and tries to do it, the information can get mixed up, and there can be issues with missed information or misreading it. Having machine learning go through and check out that information, and then using that information to make predictions for the company based on that data will make a big difference in speed and accuracy.

Of course, it is possible if you would like to, it is possible to have someone go through this information and try to figure out to make predictions. But for larger companies, this is going to be a ton of information, and often too much for the person to do efficiently. They could feel confused and overwhelmed about all the information, they may not know the best way to search through all the information and start, and it is easy to miss out on some stuff when there is so much information.

Plus, when there are hundreds of thousands of data points to sift through, it can take the individual way too long to go through it, and the information could be outdated by the time they are done. Machine learning instead is going to be able to take on all of the work and can get the results and predictions back in a fraction of the time. This is why so many companies enjoy working with machine learning. They like to add this into their business model to help them understand their customers and make the right decisions for their futures.

Now that we have learned more about machine learning, and how it is similar to and different from the ideas of artificial intelligence, you can see how these are entirely different from one another. Now, it is time to take that information and look at how to add in statistics to the mix and see more about how machine learning can work for you.

Chapter 3: Can I Use Probability and Statistics to Help Me with Machine Learning?

As you start to work with the process of machine learning, it is essential to know that there is going to be a friendly relationship that ends up showing between this process, and what is called the probability theory. Machine learning is a pretty broad field to work with, and this means that it doesn't work on its own, but also with some other fields at the same time. The fields you will be able to work with often depend on the kind of project.

One thing that you are going to notice when you start with machine learning is that it can merge with statistics and probability. It is so crucial for a lot of the projects that you choose to start on to learn how these three different areas are going to work together.

Now, there are a few different methods that you can utilize with the probability and statistics, and all of them are important to the learning process that you need to see happen here. The first thing to consider is picking out the right algorithm. And as you go through this guidebook, you will find that there are a lot of different algorithms that you can use, including supervised, unsupervised, and also reinforced learning algorithms. However, not all of the algorithms are going to work with every project that you have.

When you pick out one of the algorithms to work with (and we will talk about quite a few of these in this guidebook), there are a few things you need to balance out together, including the number of parameters that you need, the complexity, the training time that you can work with, and the accuracy. As we spend more time with machine learning, you will find that each project you need to focus on will ask for a specific combination of these factors, so consider that ahead of time.

When you decide to work with the ideas of statistics and the probability theory, you will be better prepared to pick out the parameters that are right for your specific program, the strategies for validation, and you can then use all of these to pick out the algorithm for this project. This is also going to be helpful to use when you want to figure out the amount of uncertainty that is present in that algorithm, and then you can determine if there is a level of trust that you should have for any predictions.

As you can imagine here, both of these two topics are going to be very useful when working on any project with machine learning, and they will do wonders when you want to understand what is going on with any project. This chapter will look at the different topics that come with both statistics and the probability theory, and how you can use them on any project.

What are the random variables?

Now, the first topic in statistics is random variables. With probability theory, these random variables are going to be expressed with the "X" symbol, and it is the variable that has all its possible variables come out as numerical outcomes that will come up during one of your random experiments. With random variables, there are going to be either continuous or discrete options. This means that sometimes, your random variables will be functions that will map outcomes to the real value inside their space. We will look at a few examples of this one to help it make sense later on.

We are going to start with an example of a random variable by throwing a die. The random variable that we are going to look at is going to be represented by X, and it will rely on the outcome that you will get once the die is thrown. The choices of X that would come naturally here is going to go through to map out the outcome denoted as 1 to the value of i.

What this means is that if X equals 1, you will map the event of throwing a one on your die to being the value of i. You would be able to map this out with any number that is on the die, and it is even possible to take it to the next step and pick out some mappings that are a bit strange. For example, you could map out Y to make it the outcome of 0. This can be a hard process to do, and we aren't going to spend much time on it, but it can help you to see how it works. When we are ready to write out this one, we would have the probability, which is shown as P of outcome 1 of random variable X. it would look like the following:

PX(i) or (x=i)

Distribution

Now that we have looked a bit at the random variables, it is time to look a bit at the idea of a probability distribution, and how it works with machine learning. What is meant here is that we need to take a look at the outcomes and figure out the probability that they are going to happen, or a random variable to happen. To make this even easier, we are going to use this distribution to figure out how likely it is that we are going to get a specific number.

Let's say that you are working with a die. There are six sides on it, and you have a random probability of one of the numbers showing up each time that you throw it. We can use the distribution to figure out how likely it is that with a particular throw, we will get a five or a two or one of the other numbers.

To help us get started with this one, it helps to have an example. We will need to let the X, which is our random variable, but the outcome that we will see on the die when we throw it. We are also going to start this experiment using the assumption that the die is perfectly capable of being used, with no tricks, and it isn't loaded. This ensures that the sides all end up with the same probability of showing up each time that you do a throw. The probability distribution you will work with here to figure out how probable it is that one number will show up includes

PX(1) = PX(2) = ... = PX(6) = 1/6

In this example, it matches up to what we did with the random variables. It does have a different meaning. Your probability distribution is more about the spectrum of events that can happen, while our random variable example is all about which variables are there. With the probability theory, the P(X) part is going to note that we are working with our probability distribution of the random variable X.

While you take a look at this example, you may notice that your distribution could have just one variable, or there could be two or more of these variables that show up at the same time. When this occurs, you will name it a joint distribution. To figure out this probability, you will need to figure out the variables on their own and combine them to see the results.

To see how this is going to work when it comes to two or more variables, let's have X be the random variable and the one that will be defined by the outcome you can get any time you throw the die. And then you can use Y to show us the random variable that will tell you what results occur if you decide to flip a coin. For this one, to make things easier, we are going to assign the heads side of the coin 1, and the tails side is going to be 0. This is used to help us figure out the probability distribution for each variable on their own and together.

We are going to denote this joint distribution as P(X, Y) and the probability of X as having an outcome of a and Y as having an outcome of b as either P(x =a, Y =b) or PX, Y(a,b).

Conditional distribution

The next thing we need to bring into the mix with machine learning and statistics is the idea of the conditional distribution. When we already know what the random variable distribution is all about, possibly because we already know the value of the second random variable, then we can base the probability of one event on the outcome we can get with that second event. So, you will find that when you use this distribution, you will have the random variable be known as X when X -2 given that the variable of Y is going to be Y = b. When these are true, the following formula is going to help you to define and figure out what the variable is for both of the situations:

$$P(X = a | Y = b) = P(X = a, Y = b)/P(Y = b).$$

As you work through machine learning, there are going to be a few times when you may need to use conditional distributions. These can be useful tools depending on the system that you are designing, especially if you need to have the program reason with uncertainty.

Independence

And finally, when working with statistics and probability during machine learning, we need to consider independence. One of the variables that you can work with here is to figure out how much independence is inside the problem. When you work with these random variables, you are going to find out that they are going to be independent of what the other random variables are, as long as the distribution that you have doesn't change if you take a new variable and try to add it into that equation.

To make this one work a bit better, you are going to need to work with a few assumptions in concerns to the data you are using with machine learning. This makes it a bit easier when you already know about independence. An excellent example to help us understand what this is all about is a training sample that uses j and I, and are independent of any underlying space when the label of sample I is unaffected by the features sample j. No matter what one of the variables turns out, the other one is not going to see any change or be affected, if they are independent.

Think back to the example of the die and the coin flip. It doesn't matter what number shows up on the die. The coin is going to have its result. And the same can be said the other way around as well. The X random variable is always going to be independent of the Y variable. It doesn't matter the value of Y, but the following code needs to be true for it:

$P(X) = P(X|Y)$.

In the case above, the values that come up for X and Y variables are dropped because, at this point, the values of these variables are not going to matter that much. But with the statement above, it is true for any value that you provide to your X or Y, so it isn't going to matter what values are placed in this equation.

This chapter went over a few of the things that you can do with the help of probability theory and statistics when you are working on machine learning. You can experiment with some of these to get the hang of what you can do using them, and then we can learn a few more algorithms that you can use later on.

Chapter 4: How Do I Learn the Building Blocks to Be Successful with Machine Learning?

Before we start to take a look at the different machine learning algorithms that are out there, we divide them up into the three main sections to make things easier; we need to take a look at some of the important building blocks when it comes to doing well with machine learning.

There are going to be some crucial algorithms that you will want to learn all about, and how to use them to ensure that you see the best results with any projects you do in machine learning. Before that, it is important to learn a few of the basic building blocks of machine learning to make things easier. Doing this is going to help you when working with any of these algorithms.

As you learn more about this process and get more into making your projects, you will find that these algorithms are going to be so awesome to work with. These algorithms, when you use them properly, can do a lot of amazing things in machine learning. And they are often seen as the main reason why you would want to use this process.

But before we get to all of these algorithms and explore all of the fantastic things that come with it, we need to learn a few basics of machine learning. These will include things like learning the framework that comes with machine learning, and some of the underlying topics that will make sure you get your expected result.

The learning framework

If you remember back to the previous chapter, you will most likely remember that we spent some time talking about all of the statistics that often go with machine learning. When you use some of the contexts that we spent time on before, it is easier to simplify the whole process of learning your computer will go through. If this sounds confusing, let's look at an example to help us get started.

For this example, let's say that you want to visit a new island and go on a vacation. You go there, and the natives from there seem like they enjoy eating some papaya regularly. You want to have some to try as well and would like to enjoy it as well, but since your experience with this food is limited, it is hard to know which ones are going to taste good, and which ones you won't like. But, despite this, you still want to give it a try, and you make your way to the marketplace in the hopes of figuring out the best tasting one.

There are a few different options that you can use to look at the papayas and figure out the one that is going to work the best for you, the one you like the most. You could start this process by going down to the marketplace and asking around, finding out the opinion of those around to see if you will find the right one. Of course, for each person you ask, you are likely to get a lot of answers as well.

Another option to rely on is your experiences with fruits in the past. At one point or another, you have purchased some fruit at the store. You probably have a method that you like to use to make picking out the fruit a bit easier. You could use these same ideas to help you look through the papaya that is available at the market, and make your decision.

Once you get to the supermarket, you can take a look at the papaya, maybe noticing the color, and the softness of the fruit to make the best decisions. As you take a look at these fruits though, you will notice that they come in many different colors from reds to browns. And they have a variety when it comes to how soft and hard they are. This can make it even more confusing to know what is going to work or not.

So, you look around to see what is there, and in the process, you decide to come up with a model to help you learn the best papaya, so you are prepared for the next time you come to the market. This model you are going to make here, which is in a simplified form with the fruits, will be known as a formal statistical learning framework. There will be four components that we are going to focus on with this framework, and they include:

1. Some simple data generalization

2. A measure of how successful it is

3. The output from the learner

4. And the input from the learner

Each of these four parts will be important when it comes to helping us figure out which papaya we like the most. And the more variety and information you feed to this in the beginning, the more accurate your results are going to be the next time that you head to the marketplace. Let's take a look at what each of these components is all about, so you can make the right decisions.

The input of the learner

The first section of the framework that you need to look at is called the learner's input. To do this, you need to find a domain set and then focus on it. This domain can be an arbitrary set, found in the objects, which in this framework is known as the points, that you need to label. So, going back to the exercise about the papaya, you would have the domain set to be any of the papayas that you are checking out. Then the domain points would be able to use the vectors of features, which in this case, includes the softness and color of the fruit.

Once you have determined what domain points and domain sets you want to use, you can then go through and create the label set you will use. In this exercise, the label set is going to hold onto the predictions you will make about the papayas. You can look at each papaya, and then predict how it tastes and whether it is the best one for you.

The label set from this exercise will have two elements. The X is going to be any of the papayas that you think are going to taste bad. And then, the Y is going to be the ones that you feel taste the best.

From here, you can work on what is known as the training data. This training data is going to be a set which can hold the sequence pairs that you will use when testing the accuracy of your predictions. So, with the exercise of the papayas, the training data will be the papayas that you decide to purchase. You will then take these home, and taste them to see what tastes the best. This can help you to make better decisions later on when you purchase papayas. If you find that you like a specific softness or color, you will ensure that you purchase that kind the next time.

The output of the learner

Once you have gone through and figured out the input of your learner, it is time to figure out what your output will be, based on that same input. This output is going to be used to help you create a prediction on what you will like, and what you will want to avoid. There are a few different names you may hear it being called, including classifier, predictor, and hypothesis, and you are going to use these to take the domain points and label them.

So, going back to the example that we have done with the papaya, this rule is going to be the standard, which you are going to set at the best place for you. You can then use this standard to make it easier to figure out whether any given papaya is going to taste good or not before you purchase it the next time you head to the market.

Now, when you decide to get started with this, you are making some guesses. You have never had papaya before, so figuring out which one is the best will take some trial and error. Of course, it is perfectly fine to bring in some of the experiences that you have from the past to help out with this if you would like. But, given the fact that you haven't had papaya in the past, you may be wrong about your assumptions in the beginning.

The best way for this example to get output is to make some guesses based on your past experiences with fruits, and then take a bite and see if you were right. If you can pick out a lot of different papayas, and try out a bite or two of each one, you will quickly be able to figure out which one tastes the best to you, and from there, you can look at its characteristics, and make a decision based on that.

Using the data generalization model

Once you have gone through this example, or any machine learning example that you would like to work with, and you have figured out what the input and the output of the learner are going to be, it is time to work with the data generalization model. This is an excellent model to work with because it ensures you can create some training data to use, and this data is going to be based on the probability distribution of the domain sets that you decide to use with the papayas.

We are still sticking with the papayas here. In this example, you will find that the model you need to focus on is going to be any method that you would like to use to help you figure out the best-tasting papaya. It can help you figure out what to grab at the market, so you can bring home some variety and figure out what tastes good later.

Of course, the distribution is hard to figure out when you have never worked with papaya, or with the given data, in the past. But using this data generalization model is going to help you get a better distribution of the data, and can make it easier to pick out the right kinds of papaya from the beginning.

How to measure the success

Now, while the data generalization model is a great one to work with, you are not able to work with this model until you have found a way to measure out whether you were successful or not. You need to put in place a method that will make it easier to know whether or not you were successful with this particular product.

The good news with this is that there are quite a few options that are available for you to choose from. But since there are a good number of options in papayas to choose from, you need to have some indicator in place along the way that can help with predictions and success when it is time to make your selections.

Remember that the main goal that comes with this experiment is to help you as the user figure out from all of the different options, the fruit that will taste the best. When you figure this out, you can then keep that information in mind to pick out the right papayas to use in the future.

Since there is a good deal of variety when it comes to the softness, the shape, and the color of the papaya, you may find that picking out a good sample, different softness and different colors can be the best bet for you. You can then taste each one, and write down what your observations were so that you are more likely to head back and grab the right ones the next time if you choose.

If you go through this and only grab one or two of the fruits, and there are twenty different kinds there, you are reducing the odds that you are going to find a type you like. Maybe none of those two taste good. Maybe they taste fine to you, but there is one in the mix that would taste even better, but you haven't had a chance to taste it yet. This is why having a wide sample size can make it more likely that you get accurate results.

PAC strategies of learning

Now that we know the four main components that come with the idea of machine learning, and we know how to set up our hypothesis, and how to set up your training data, it is time to look at something that is known as PAC learning. There are going to be two main parameters that are important to this learning, and they include the output classifier and the accuracy parameter.

To help us get started with this one, we need to focus on the accuracy parameter first. This parameter is important because it is going to be used by the user to determine how often the output classifier you are setting up, in the beginning, will be able to make predictions that are the right ones. You need to have these predictions set up so that they can look at the information you are providing, and then make the right predictions.

You can also take some time to work on the confidence parameter when you are in machine learning. This is another important parameter because it will measure how likely it is that your predictor will be able to reach the level of accuracy that you would like. Depending on the data you are using, and the situation that you find yourself in, accuracy is going to be important. You want to make sure that any algorithm you choose to go with can be fairly high when it comes to accuracy. Otherwise, how are you supposed to know that your information is true or will work out the best for your needs?

As you work with machine learning, you will find that there are several different ways that you can utilize these PAC learning options, and they can come in handy when you are doing a project. You may want to use this learning any time you work with training data to help you see whether you are getting the accuracy you want. You may want to use it, and have it go along with machine learning when you are worried about uncertainties that will come up in the data.

The PAC strategies for learning in machine learning are going to be very useful when it comes to helping you get the results that you would like out of the project. We will take a look at a few algorithms that will work well with this as we progress through this book, but learning their basics now can prepare you when your project needs this thing to show up.

Generalization models that can help out with machine learning

Any time you are working with machine learning, and you are considering all about the generalization of the project, you are going through and seeing that there are at least two components present there, and that you need to work with both of these components before you can accurately and efficiently get through the data that you have. The components that you need to focus on for these generalizations include the rate of error that is true and the reliability assumption.

One thing that you should look for is whether or not you can work with those two components, and you are also able to meet with the reliability assumption; it is a good thing. When these happen, you can expect that the algorithm you are using here is going to be reliable, and will give you the distribution and the results that you would like.

With that said, there are also going to be times when the assumption that you try to make with these generalizations ends up not being all that practical. This means that the standards you ended up picking may have turned out unrealistic, or you went through and chose the wrong algorithm when it was time to get the work done.

There are a lot of algorithms that you can focus on when you are doing machine learning. And the type that you decide to go with on one of your projects doesn't always guarantee that the hypothesis it comes up with will turn out to be something you agree with or like. Unlike using the Bayes predictor (which we will talk about more in a bit), which is a good algorithm to use for many of the predictions that you want to make, these algorithms are not going to be set up in the right way to find out which error rate is the best.

You have to choose the algorithm that you want to use very carefully. There are some projects that you will want to focus on that have a set and easy algorithm. You can look at it and know right away what algorithm you should use. But then, there are some of those projects that more than one will work, or you have to figure out which one is going to work the best, and this is where some trouble can come in.

Sometimes, there isn't a cut and dry answer that you can work with, and you have to make an educated guess as to which one is going to work the best for you. And then, there are times when you will need to try out two of them and figure out whether they cross over at some point, and use that as your basis here. As you get more into machine learning, you will be able to learn what works the best for you, and you can continue to use this on any project that you want.

When you are doing anything in machine learning, there will be times, no matter how hard you try to fight against it or hope that it doesn't happen, you will need to make some assumptions to move things along. And in these cases, working with your prior experience, the ones that are similar to what you are dealing with now can help to move the process along and get accurate results. And then, like with the example of our papayas above, you may have some times when you need to experiment to figure out what is the best course of action. But no matter which method or algorithm or anything else that you need to go with, you will be able to use machine learning to make this easier.

And there you have it! These are some of the most basic building blocks that you will need to know when it is time to understand more about machine learning. Keeping these in mind, and reviewing them before you decide to start on some of your projects will help you to get the most out of your machine learning experience.

These basic building blocks may sound like they are going to be a waste of time, and you may not understand how they are going to work in your projects, they are so important here. You will be able to work with these simple building blocks to see how programs are run, and thanks, machine learning is working. You will then be able to see how this information is used in the following chapters as we talk more about some of the algorithms used in machine learning.

Chapter 5: What Is Supervised Machine Learning?

So far in this guidebook, we have discussed machine learning and some of the amazing things that you can do with it.

Now that we have some of the basics things about machine learning and how to use it, it is time to move on to some of the machine learning you can work with, and even some of the algorithms that also work well with this.

To start with, in this chapter, there are three main types of machine learning that programmers can use.

The three main types, including the one we will explore in this chapter, include supervised, unsupervised, and reinforcement learning.

All of these are going to be a part of machine learning, but they are going to work in different ways to help you get the results you need for your project. The one type that you will want to work with often depends on the type of project, as you will see as we explore them a bit more.

First, we need to take a look at the most basic machine learning known as supervised machine learning. Supervised learning is the type that occurs when you choose one of the algorithms that can learn the right responses to any given data. There are a few different ways that supervised machine learning can work with this. You will find that supervised learning is amazing, and let's look at an example, along with some other targeted responses, that you set to the computer. You could also spend some time adding values or other strings of labels to help the program learn the way you want it to behave.

This is a pretty simple process that you can work with. But an excellent way to look at this is when we look at a classroom.

A teacher may choose to show their students a brand new topic, and one method of doing this is to show the class of students some examples of the situation that is going on.

Through this method, the students are going to learn how to memorize these examples because they know that these examples are going to provide them with some general rules to follow. Any time they see these examples, along with other examples similar to what they were shown, they know how to respond.

However, if they see an example that isn't similar to what they were shown in class, they also know how to respond in this situation.

There are several types of learning algorithms you can use when in supervised machine learning.

But the most common types and the ones that we are going to explore in this chapter will include:

1. Random forests

2. Regression algorithms

3. KNN

4. Decision trees

Decision trees

The first algorithm to consider with supervised machine learning is the decision trees. These are nice to work with because they are efficient data tools any time you would like to look at the different scenarios provided, and then pick out the right options for these for your business. Once the decision tree can present you with a few options, you can see the outcomes and the possibilities that come with them. And all of this information can be used to help you make the most accurate and helpful predictions for your needs.

It is also possible to use these decision trees for either continuous random variables, or when you want to work with categorical variables. However, most of the time, when you decide to work with these decision trees, you are working with classification problems.

For a programmer to make a good decision tree, it is vital to take all of the data and split it up into domains, and then you will split it up into a minimum of two sets even though you will often get more of similar data. These data sets are going to be sorted out with the help of their independent variables because it will make it easier also to distinguish the different sets that you are working with.

So, we have talked about these a bit here, but it is time to get a better idea of how this works. For this example, we are going to assume that there are 60 people in the group. Out of these 60, there are going to be three independent variables to consider including their gender, which class they are in, and their heights.

When we take a look at all of these people in the group, we know from the start that half of them, or 30 people like to spend some of their time playing soccer. So, with this knowledge, we decide to work on a model that will help us to figure better out which of the students are soccer players, and enjoy playing this sport, and which ones aren't.

To help us to figure this out, we need to work on a decision tree, one that can look at the people in the group and divide them up based on their similarities and more. We would use the three variables that we talked about before. If the decision tree works out the way we would like, or hope is that we are going to find a set of students that can end up homogenous when it is all said and done.

Of course, there are some other algorithms that you can use to figure this one out. And some of them are going to work well with the decision tree to ensure that you can accurately split up your data. This is to ensure that you are going to end up with two subsets at a minimum, and the outcomes are going to end up homogenous. It is possible to have more of these, but since we are just trying to figure out whether we have a person in the group who likes to play soccer or not, right now, we are going to work on dividing the students up into two groups, whether they play soccer or not.

Decision trees can be an excellent option for you when considering supervised machine learning. This is because these decision trees will allow you to take the data and split them up. Then, with this data split up and ready to go, you can look it over and make some decisions. It is a great way to ensure you are making the best decisions for your business and yourself because all of the information is going to be in front of you, sorted out and easy to read, rather than having to look at all of the conflicting information, and make an educated guess in the process.

Random forests

There are a lot of situations where you can use the decision tree to make some of the decisions and sort the data that you want.

But there are also times when it isn't going to do the work the right way. If you are looking at your data and you know that the decision tree isn't the right option for you, then you may find that the random forest is a bit better to work with.

These random forests can be popular to use, and if you plan to do a lot of work in the field of data science, then you will want to learn more about these and how you can use them in your needs. Since these algorithms are well-known in the industry, you will find that many people use them to solve various problems that come up. For example, if you would like to work on a task that will explore through all the data you have, such as dealing with some of the values that may have gone missing, or dealing with any of the information outliers that show up, these random forests are going to be there to help you get it all done.

Now, you may find that as you work on machine learning, there will be some times when you will use them because they seem to be the perfect option for giving you great results, results that other algorithms are just not able to do.

Some of the different advantages that you can get in random forests will include:

1. When you decide to create some of your training sets and work on these, you may find that all of the objects inside that set will be generated randomly. You will be able to replace this if your random tree works the right way, and can help you to sort through the information based on your needs.

2. If there are M input variable amounts, then m<M is going to be specified from the beginning, and it will be held as a constant. The reason this is so important is that each tree you have is randomly picked from their variable using M.

3. The goal of each of your random trees will be to find the best split for variable m.

4. As the tree grows, all of these trees are going to keep getting as big as they possibly can. Remember that these random trees are not going to prune themselves.

5. The forest that is created from a random tree can be great because it is much better at predicting specific outcomes. It can do this for you because it will take all prediction from each of the trees that you create, and then select the average for regression or the consensus that you get during classification.

You may find that it is great to work with random forests any time you are doing things in data science, and there are going to be quite a few advantages to working with a random forest rather than some of the other algorithms, even though it isn't going to be perfect each time. Just because the random variable can provide you with a lot of the results that you would like, you do have to know when it can be useful, and when it should be avoided. With that said, there are some advantages to its use.

First, these random forests are good to use because they can work with regression and classification problems that you have. Many other algorithms are not able to work with both of these. Also, you may find that random forests are a good option to go with if you are handling large amounts of data because you can add in hundreds of data points and variables, and the random forest will still be able to handle this.

One thing to consider when you are working with this is that while the random forest can handle a lot of regression problems, they will have some issues with predictions. Random forests are not going to be limited in this because they are not able to go past any of the ranges that you provide to them so there may be times when your accuracy is not going to be as high as you would like.

The KNN algorithm

The third supervised machine learning algorithm you can work with is known as the KNN algorithm. This one is also known as the k-nearest neighbor's algorithm.

When you decide to use this algorithm, it is going to be helpful to take all of your data, the data you have for k most similar examples of any instance of data that you are working on.

Once you see some success with this, the KNN algorithm will then be able to go through all of your data points and provide you with a summary of all the results. Many companies and programmers can use this to help them look through the results and make some good predictions.

Any time you plan to work with this KNN algorithm model, you will be able to see it as a form of competitive learning. This is going to work well because the different elements will end up competing against one another. This may sound like a bad thing, but when the elements start to compete against one another, they become better at making successful predictions.

As you can imagine, this one is going to work a bit different than the other algorithms that we have talked about in this guidebook so far. Some programmers don't like to use it because they think that KNN is more of a lazy learning process. This is because while it can be effective at providing you with some results, it isn't going to help you out by creating any models until you specifically ask for a brand new prediction. This can be good sometimes, but it will depend on the case. Some people want it to make new predictions automatically, and some like that they will have the most relevant information for the task at hand.

Different benefits can come when you decide to work with this KNN algorithm. When you choose to go with this algorithm, you can cut through a lot of the noise found inside your specific set of data.

This is because the KNN algorithm is going to rely more on a competitive method to sort through all of the data that you see. This algorithm is going to be great when you want to handle a lot of data, so it is one that you should consider if your data is pretty large. At the same time, it works well if you need some help sorting through all of this data.

Now, you could have someone go through and look at all this information, providing you with some estimations and predictions for you as well. But this is not that efficient with large forms of data. Sure, it can be done, but it can take a long time, often so long that new data is coming in and the predictions you have will be too old to work with. It can also lead to more mistakes as someone could also miss information or misread. The KNN algorithm can solve this problem by taking out the human error and sorting through any amount of data that you would like.

One of the biggest problems that you are going to see when you decide to work with the KNN algorithm is that the costs of computing the information are going to be pretty high, especially when you try to compare it to some of the algorithms. This is because this algorithm is meant to take a look at all of the data points that you have, every one before it sends out the prediction that you want. This sometimes provides more accurate predictions and information, but the computational costs may be too high for some people.

The Naïve Bayes

The next machine learning we are considering here is known as the Naïve Bayes. To start this one, let's turn on our imaginations a bit to help us to understand how this one is going to work.

Here, we need to imagine that we are doing some machine learning work, and our scenario is going to be that we need to do problems of classification. In the process, we want to be able to create a brand new hypothesis, as well as design some new discussions and features that will be based on the importance given to each variable.

Once we gather and use this information, it is likely that, even though it is early on in the process, the stakeholders of that company are going to want to look at the models and see what is going on. Of course, at this early stage, it is not likely that you will have that information ready to present. So, how are you supposed to make the stakeholders happy and provide them with the information they want if you aren't done with it yet?

In many cases, you are starting this process with hundreds of thousands of data points that you need to go through, and all of these need to be shown in the model. In addition to this, there are going to be a lot of other variables that can show up in this training set as well. This is a lot of information to throw together quickly, especially if you haven't been able to sort through it all. And it is likely that your stakeholders are not data scientists and won't be able to read through all of that information by having you throw it on a screen in front of them. How are you able to take this information and show it to your stakeholders and present it in a way they will understand.

The good news is with this scenario, there is a good algorithm that a data scientist is able to work with to help out, and can ensure that you are able to stick with some of the earlier stages of the model, while still showing the information off easily for others to understand.

And all of this can be done while showing all the information you need. The algorithm that works the best for this is going to be called the Naïve Bayes algorithm, and it is one of the best ways to use a few demonstrations to showcase your model, even when you are still in some of the earliest stages of development.

Let's take a look at how this is going to work by looking at an example with apples. When you grab a normal looking apple, you should be able to state some of the features that are the most distinguishable. This could include that your apple is red or green, that it is round, and it is going to come in around three inches. While some of these features are also going to be found in other fruit types, when all of these features are present together, then we know how the fruit we are holding is a fruit.

Now, this may seem to be a pretty basic way to think and look at things, but it is a good way to understand how the Naïve Bayes formula is going to work. The model of Naïve Bayes is meant to be easy for anyone, whether they are a programmer or not, to put together, and sometimes, it is going to be used to help you look through large data sets. Sometimes, it is easier to work with this model compared to some of the other models out there, even if they are more sophisticated.

As you start to learn more about machine learning and the Naïve Bayes algorithm, you will find that there were going to be a lot of reasons and situations when using it. This model is straightforward to use, and it is effective when predicting the class of your test data sets, so it is a great choice for someone who wants to keep things simple or new to the whole process. Even though this is a simple algorithm to use, this model is still going to perform well, and it has proven that it can do a job better than some of the higher class algorithms in some cases.

You do need to be careful with this one though because there are some negatives to using the Naïve Bayes' algorithm. First, when you are working with categorical variables, and you need to test data that hasn't been through the training data set, you will find that this model is not able to make a perfect prediction for you and will assign those data sets a 0 probability. You can add in some other methods that will help to solve this issue, such as the Laplace estimation, but it can be confusing for someone who is brand new to working in machine learning.

This is not going to be the method you use all of the time, but if you have a lot of information that you are working on, and you need to showcase it in a simplified manner for your shareholders or anyone else, then working with the Naïve Bayes algorithm is the best option for you.

Regression algorithms

Another algorithm that works well with machine learning is called a regression analysis. This is going to be the type that you can use when you want to look through your predictor variables and any dependent variables and whether there is a relationship between them. You will see that this is a good technique that you can work with when figuring out if there is a causal relationship between the variable, the time series modeling, and the forecasting you are using.

The point of using a regression algorithm is that it should take all of the information that you have, and fits it on a line or a curve, as much as it can. This helps you to see the common factors that show up in your data. This is a good way to help you figure out whether some similarities show up in your information or data points or not.

Many companies will use the regression algorithm to help them make great predictions that will increase their profits. You will be able to use it to come up with a great estimation of the sales growth for the company while still basing it on how the economic conditions in the market are doing right at this moment.

The great thing about this is that you can add in any information that you would like to use. You can add in information about the past and the current economy to this particular algorithm, such as your past and current economic information, and then this gives you an idea of how the growth is going to go in the future. Of course, you do need to have the right information about the company to make this happen.

For example, if you use the regression algorithm and find that your company is growing at the same rate as what other industries are doing in the economy, you would then be able to use this information to help make predictions for how your company will do in the future if the economy does end up changing.

As you are working with this algorithm in machine learning, there are going to be a few enjoyable variations. You have to learn how each one can be used, so you know whether or not it will work for your particular project or not. There are many variations of this algorithm that are available for you to use, but some of the most common options are going to include:

1. Stepwise regression
2. Ridge regression
3. Polynomial regression
4. Linear regression
5. Logistic regression

When you are working with these regression algorithms, you will easily be able to take a look to see that there is a nice relationship present with your dependent and your independent variables. This algorithm is also going to help you know what impact will show up if you try to add in or change some of the variables that show up in the data.

Even though this is a great option to work with, it is important to note that there are a few shortcomings that will show up with it. The biggest shortcoming is that this algorithm is not very good at helping with classification problems. The main reason for this one is that it is too hard to try and overfit the data that you have in many situations. So, any time you would like to change up the constraints that you are using with this, the whole process is going to be tedious to get done.

As you can see from this chapter, there are quite a few different algorithms that you can use when it comes to machine learning, even when you are using the supervised machine learning variety. These are going to be pretty simple ones, where you teach the computer how to behave and work up from there. The computer or the program will then be able to use some of the information that it has gathered throughout the time, and from the past, to make informed predictions about what will happen in the future.

Supervised machine learning does have some parts that are lacking. But you will find that it is a great way to ensure the program can do some of the learning needed on its own. Also, the type of algorithm that you are going to use will depend on the application and the project you have to get done. After reading through this chapter, you should have a better idea of whether this is the right machine learning algorithm for you, and which one would be able to help you out here.

Chapter 6: Unsupervised Machine Learning

Now that we have explored a bit about supervised machine learning, it is time to explore other options that you can work with when it comes to machine learning. The first one that we spent some time talking about was supervised learning. As we discussed, supervised learning is designed in a way where you will show the computer some examples, and then you teach that computer how you would like it to respond based on the given examples.

There are going to be a lot of programs where this technique is going to end up working well for you.

But, when you think about showing hundreds or thousands of different examples to your computer, it is all going to seem pretty tedious.

And then there are times when the program isn't going to be able to learn this way and still give you the expected results. This is where the other two types of machine learning are going to come into play.

This is where you will find unsupervised machine learning is going to come into play. This chapter is going to spend some more time talking about unsupervised machine learning and what it is all about. Unsupervised machine learning is going to be a type of learning that is going to happen if your algorithm makes mistakes and can learn from these mistakes along the way. And the program can do it even without having an associated response to work from.

This may sound a bit confusing, but it is going to be when you can teach the computer through trial and error, without it having to work with a million examples to make sure it behaves how you would like it to do. With these different algorithms, it is possible they figure out and analyze the patterns in the data based on any provided input from you or the user.

The good news here is that there are going to be a few different algorithm types that you can work with when you decide to choose unsupervised machine learning. The algorithm that you choose to work with is going to take the data that you have, and it will restructure it so that the data can fall into one of your classes.

These classes are nice because they make it easier for you to see the information nice and sorted out, and it makes it so much easier for you to look through the information later on. There are many times when you will use this machine learning because it can set up your computer, or another device, to do most of the work of learning, without having a person sit there and writing out all of the instructions. The computer will do some trial and error and figure out how it should act over time.

Let's take a look at an example. If you have a company that has a considerable amount of data that they want to read through, such as data they want to use to make predictions and make decisions about how to act in the future, then you may want to work with machine learning. You don't want to have one or two people go through this information. It would take up too much time and effort to get this all done. But unsupervised machine learning is going to do the work for you. Search engines also often use unsupervised machine learning.

Working with unsupervised learning

Before we get too far into some of the techniques that can be used with unsupervised machine learning, it is essential to understand a little bit about it. When you are working in a real-world environment, there are going to be times when your machine, either in artificial intelligence or a robotic role, won't be able to access the optimal answer with the information that you provided. Maybe there isn't even an optimal answer to the question. You want to make sure that this robot or machine can explore the world all on its own, and learn how to do things just by taking a look at the patterns available.

In most cases, unsupervised learning is for learning the structure, or even the probability distribution of data. But what does this mean? We are going to spend some time talking about some of the different examples where you can use unsupervised learning to help get things done.

There are a few different ways you will be able to work with unsupervised learning. Often, it is to help the computer or the machine find the answers or needed results, without you having to explain it out. With unsupervised learning, the computer is going to learn how to behave based on past performance and feedback. This can be nice because you will be able to insert the information that you want, and the computer will do the work.

Density Estimation

You should know at this point that we use the probability density function, or PDF, to tell us the probability that will occur of a random variable.

Density estimation is the process of taking samples of data of the random variable and figuring out the probability density function.

After you learn the distribution of the variable, you will be able to use machine learning to generate your samples of the variable based on this information.

For example, at a higher level, you could take Shakespeare and learn its distribution. You can then take this information and generate out a text that looks very similar to what you would find with Shakespeare.

Latent Variables

Many times, you will want to know some of the underlying or the hidden causes of the data you are looking at. You can consider these hidden, missing, or latent variable. For example, say that someone gives you a set of documents, but they don't tell you what these documents are. You would be able to use the clustering option with machine learning to find out that there are a few distinct groups of information in the document. The machine learning would be able to tell you this information rather than you having to read through it all.

After you have done clustering, you can read through a few of the documents in this data set and find out that maybe one is children's books, one is a romance novel, and so on. There are several different types of clustering that you can work with. You would use this information any time when the data is too big that it doesn't make sense to go through all of it on your own. The clustering process will be able to summarize the data to help you sort it all out.

There are a few different techniques that you can use when it is time to work with machine learning of this kind. Some of the methods or the algorithms that tend to work the best here are going to include:

1. Neural networks
2. Markov algorithm
3. Clustering algorithm

Let's explore each of these topics and learn a bit more about how they are all going to work, and some of the basics of when and how you are going to be able to use them for your own needs with machine learning.

Clustering algorithms

The first machine learning that we will look at is called the clustering algorithm. With the clustering algorithm, we are going to keep it pretty simple. This method can take our data and then classify it into clusters. Before the program even starts, you get the benefit of picking out how many clusters you would like all the information to fit into. For example, you may decide that you want to combine the data into five different clusters. The program would then go through and divide up all the information you have into five different clusters so that you could look through it.

The beautiful thing about this algorithm is that it is responsible for doing most of the work for you. This is because it is in charge of how many of your data points are going to fit into those clusters that you chose. To keep things organized, we are going to call all of the main clusters that you picked cluster centroids.

So, when you are looking at one of your clusters, and you notice that there are a lot of points inside of it, you can safely assume that all those particular data points have something in common or they are similar. There is some attribute or another that all the data points in one cluster have in common with each other.

Once these original clusters are formed, you can take each of the individual ones and divide them up to get more cluster sets if you would like. You can do this several times, creating more divisions as you go through the steps. You could potentially go through this enough times that the centroids will stop changing. This is when you know you are done with the process.

There are several reasons why you would want to work with a clustering algorithm to help you get a program started when doing machine learning. First, doing your computations with the help of a clustering algorithm can be easy and cost efficient, especially compared to some of the supervised learning options we earlier discussed. If you would like to do a classification problem, the clustering algorithms are efficient at getting it done.

With that said, you do need to use some caution here though. This algorithm is not going to do the work of showing predictions for you. If you end up with centroids that are not categorized the right way, then you may end up with a project that is done the wrong way.

Markov algorithm

The next type of unsupervised machine learning is the Markov algorithm. This is a nice one to use because it can take any or all of the data that you add to the system, and then translates this information so that it can work with another coding language. You will be able to set this up with any or all of the rules that you would like to be present ahead of time, based on how you would like this to work. There are times when doing this is going to be useful because it can take a string of data, and make it more useful when you learn the parameters for how your data is going to behave.

There are a lot of different ways that you can work with this Markov algorithm. One available option is if you decide to do some work with DNA. You would be able to take some of the DNA sequences that you have, and use this particular algorithm to take that information and translate it over to numerical values. When you are working with this on a computer, you will find that reading out numerical values is going to be so much easier compared to looking at a random strand of DNA, and hoping that you will be able to read through it.

You will find that a lot of programmers like to work with the Markov algorithm. A good reason to start using this one is that it is so great at learning some of the problems that you need, especially when you know the right input to use, but you are not sure about the parameters. This type of algorithm will help you find if any insights are found in your information. There are going to be times when these important insights are hidden, and this is when other algorithms are going to run into issues finding them.

There are a lot of fantastic things that come with this algorithm, but there are also going to be some downfalls that come with it as well.

There are some instances where it is difficult to work with this because you will need to go through it manually and create a new rule to use any time you are working with a new language of code.

If you only plan to use one coding language in your program, then this is not going to end up causing many issues along the way. But there are times when one program is going to need a lot of different coding languages, or if you want to work with more than one, then you will run into some trouble here and need to do some work with it. It can get tedious to come through and write out some new rules each time you want to introduce in a new coding language.

Neural networks

The next unsupervised machine learning that we are going to talk about is known as neural networks. These are going to be the networks that are used often in this because they can learn things quickly, and they are good at taking a look at a pattern and analyzing it at different layers along the way. Each layer the neural network analyzes will be dissected and will look through it to figure out what is going on, and then it puts all of the information together.

The neural network is going to make its way through each layer, checking to see if there is a pattern present inside the image. And if there is a pattern, the neural network is going to activate the process so that it can take a look at the next layer. This process will continue through this, making its way through the layers as the algorithm is created. Over time, with these predictions and looking through each layer, it will be able to make a good prediction about what is inside that image.

Now, there are a few things that can happen when you end up getting to this point of the process. If the algorithm went through these layers and was able to use that information to make accurate prediction there, these neurons are going to start becoming stronger, just like we can see in the brain. This is going to result in a good association between the patterns and the object, and the system will soon become more efficient at doing this the next time you decide to use the program.

This can sometimes seem complicated to work with, so we are going to take a bit of time here to learn more about how these work together, and why they can be so effective with machine learning. Let's say you would like to work on a new program that can take the input of a picture, and then recognize that inside the picture, there is a car. The neural networks are going to be able to do this using the features they know are in a car, including the color, the license plate, and other features.

When you are working with some of the coding methods that you can use with conventional coding methods, you will find that this is a complicated process to do. But when you add in the neural network system, then you can make this something easier to work with.

To get this algorithm to work, you have to make sure that the system, at least, has the image of a car, so it knows what to compare with. The neural network would be able to take a look at that picture of a car. It would start with the first layer, which is going to be the outside edges of the car. Then, as the neural network moves on, it is going to complete different layers of this to help the program learn the unique characteristics that are present inside that picture so that it knows what a car looks like.

Now, if you find that the program is coded the right way, and it can do its job, it is going to do a good job at finding some of the smaller details of the car. This could include some of the things like the windows, the patterns of the wheels, and so much more.

There isn't a limitation when it comes to how many layers can be present in this method. The neural network is going to try and look through as many details and layers as possible. The more that the neural network can go through, the more accurate it would be able to predict whether there is a car, and even what type of car it is.

If the neural network can accurately identify the model of the car, it can learn from this kind of lesson. The program is going to remember the patterns that it found in the picture, and it is going to store them for use if they come across this kind of pictures later. Then, the next time that the program can encounter this car model, it will predict the type of car pretty quickly.

This good algorithm is often going to be used when you would like to sort through some of the pictures that you have and learn how to sort out the different features that define it. It can be used to help with software that helps with face recognition, for example, and can be helpful if you won't be able to put in all of the information ahead of time. Some of the other things that you will be able to do with this will include - recognizing the different types of animals, defining the models of cars, and more.

One of the most significant advantages is that there won't be a lot of wasted work in statistical training for this algorithm to work for you. Even without using the statistics in this, you can find some of the complex relationships that are going to be present between the two variables, the independent and the dependent variables, even if the two of these don't end up being linear.

Of course, there are sometimes, a few drawbacks you need to be careful about when you are working with this machine learning algorithm. The biggest problem is that the neural networks are going to come with high costs of computation. This makes it hard to work with sometimes. For some companies that are high-tech and need to go through a lot of information, this can be worth it. But for other companies, this may cost too much.

Support vector machines

We also need to consider the support vector machine learning algorithms. These can also be known as SVM. The SBM is going to be used to help out with many of the challenges that you face in regression and classification, no matter what your program is trying to work on. With this one, much of the work that you try to do on these problems, especially with classification, can make the work a bit harder, but the algorithm can also help with that.

When it is time to work with the algorithm of SVM, you need to be able to take each of the items that are in the set of data, and then plot them together in one point, using the n-dimensional space. N is going to be the number of features you decide to use. Then you will look to the value of all features and how it translates to the value you find on your chosen coordinate. When you do this, your job has to be determining the hyperplane since this part will help you see the differences between the two classes you are working with.

There are also going to be a few vectors of support inside of this algorithm that you need to take note of, but you will also notice that these will end up being the coordinates of the individual observations that you end up having. You will then be able to use the SVM to be the frontier that helps you separate all of the classes. With this method, you will end up having two classes when you are all done with the hyperplane and the line.

When you reach this point, you may start to wonder what all of this means. It seems a bit complicated, and you may wonder when and why you would want to use this SVM. Taking a look at some of the ways that you would use this can also make it so much easier to use this machine learning.

The first part of this that we need to take a look at is known as the hyperplane. There are often going to be a few different types of hyperplanes with your data, and you will need to look them over and pick out which one to use. This means that you want to have a method in place to help you pick out the right one ahead of time, the one that is going to work the best for your specific needs.

This is one of the most significant issues and challenges that you need to focus on when working with the SVM algorithm in machine learning. You want to make sure you aren't wasting your time and even money with the wrong method or the wrong hyperplane, but there are often two or more that you can choose from. The good news here is that there is a process that you can choose from to help you take care of this, and increases the likelihood that you will be able to pick out the right one. The steps that you can follow to help you pick out and work with the right hyperplane includes

- We are going to start with three hyperplanes that we will call 1, 2, and 3. Then we are going to spend time figuring out which hyperplane is right so that we can classify the star and the circle.

- The good news is there is a pretty simple rule that you can follow so that it becomes easier to identify which hyperplane is the right one. The hyperplane that you want to go with will be the one that segregates your classes the best.

- That one was easy to work with, but in the next one, our hyperplanes of 1, 2, and 3 are all going through the classes, and they similarly segregate them. For example, all of the lines or these hyperplanes are going to run parallel with each other. From here, you may find that it is hard to pick which hyperplane is the right one.

- For the above issue, we will need to use what is known as the margin. This is the distance that occurs between the hyperplane and the nearest data point from either of the two classes. Then you will be able to get some numbers that can help you out. These numbers may be closer together, but they will point out which hyperplane is going to be the best.

You will find that the example above is not the only time that you will be able to work with SVM to help with this type of machine learning. When you are taking a look at the data points that you have, and you see that there is a clear margin of separation, then the SVM method is most likely the best one to use to help you out. Also, the effectiveness you get out of this model will increase any time you have a project with dimensional spaces that are pretty high. Working on this particular technique can help you use a subset of training points that come with a decision function or the support vector, and when the memory of the program you are working on is high enough to allow you to do this.

While there are benefits you will get with this method depending on the project that you are working on, there are still going to be some times when the SVM method is not the best for you. When you work with a large data set, the SVM may not provide you with the most accurate options. The training time with these larger sets of data can be high, and this will disappoint you if you need to get through the information quickly. And if some target classes are overlapping, the SVM is going to behave in a way that is different than what you want.

These are a few of the options you can choose to work with when working in machine learning that is considered unsupervised. These are a bit easier to work with, but will ensure you can get the program to work the way that you would like it to without having to go through it all, and show every example of what works and what doesn't.

Chapter 7: Reinforcement Machine Learning

Now that we have been talking about supervised and unsupervised learning, it is time to consider the third type of machine learning. This one is known as reinforcement learning, and it will make it easier for you to do a few more things in your projects that won't be done through the algorithms that we have already gone through. If the other two options are not going to work well for your needs, then it is time to bring out reinforcement machine learning.

If you haven't been able to work with machine learning at all in the past, then you may think that unsupervised learning and reinforcement learning are the same things. And they are indeed going to share a lot of similarities, but it is essential to understand that these are two different types of machine learning.

The first thing to notice is that the input given to these algorithms will need to have some mechanism in place to help with feedback. If these are not in place, the reinforcement learning is not going to work well. You can go through and set these up the way that you want. Sometimes, they will be positive, and sometimes, they will be negative based on which algorithm you would like to get started with.

So, when you decide to start bringing out reinforcement machine learning, you are working with an option that is like trial and error. When you can add in some of the trial and error, you may understand how well this learning is going to work. Think about when you are doing some work with a child. When they go through and perform an action that you are not going to approve, you will tell them to stop. Or you may have some other consequence that you use when they don't follow the directions that you want to let them know.

But, things go the other way as well. If your child does something that you approve of, something that you see as good for them, then you will make sure to give them a lot of positive reinforcement, and you will take some time to praise your child. When you do this, the positive reinforcement when they are good and the consequence when they are doing something you don't approve of, can help your child learn what they can do and what they can't.

To make this as simple as possible, the trial and error option from above is going to be similar to what you will find with reinforcement machine learning. It works on the idea that trial and error is the best way for a program to learn what it should do for each situation, and input that the user decides to work with. A reinforcement algorithm is going to be used to help your chosen program make decisions.

You will find that this learning is a great one to work with any time that you would like to bring in an algorithm that can make decisions without any mistakes and will come up with the best outcome each time. Of course, make sure that you understand that when doing this, it can take some time for the program to get accurate results because it needs to learn what you want it to do. You can add this learning to the code that you write, ensuring that the computer can learn the way that you want it to.

Now that we know a bit more about reinforcement learning and what it all entails, we need to take a look at some of the different algorithms that you can use when you want to learn this way. Some of the most common reinforcement machine learning algorithms that you can work with include:

Q-learning

There are going to be a variety of algorithms that you can work with when you need to bring in reinforcement learning that you can work with, and the first of these options is called Q-learning. This algorithm is going to work the best if you would like to work with the temporal difference learning. As you are trying to work with some of the different algorithms here, you will probably notice that this one is like an algorithm that is off-policy because it can learn an action value function. Meaning that means that no matter your state, you will get the results that you were expecting.

Since you can use this particular algorithm for any function that you want, you must go through and list out the specifications for how the user or the learner will select the course of action.

After you, the programmer, go through and then find the action value function that you want to use, then it is time to work on the optimal policy. You can work on constructing this by using the actions that will have the highest value no matter what state you are working with.

A big advantage of working with Q-learning is that you won't need to provide it with models of the environment to compare the utility of all your actions. What this means is that you can compare a few or many, actions together, and you will not need to worry about the environment that you are going to use with it.

SARSA

The other algorithm that you can work with when you are looking at a reinforcement machine learning algorithm is known as the SARSA algorithm or the state action reward state action algorithm. For this option, you are going to learn how to take the time to describe the decision process policy that will occur with that Markov algorithm that we discussed in an earlier chapter.

This would then be the primary function that you would use with the updated -value which will then rely on whatever the current state of the learner is. It can also include the reward that the learner is going to get for the selection they make, the action that the learner chooses, and then the new state that the learner is going to be in when they are done with that action. As you can see, there are a ton of different parts that will end up coming together to make the SARSA work for your needs.

While many parts must come together for this one, this is seen sometimes as the safest algorithm for a programmer to use when trying to find the solution they want to use. However, there can be times when your learner is going to end up with a reward that is higher than what the average is for their trials. This is a more significant issue with the SARSA compared to some of the other algorithms that you have.

There are also going to be times when the learner ends up not going with the optimal path either. Depending on how the program decides to react to this, it could bring up some issues with how they learn and how the program is going to behave for them.

There are some times when the reinforcement learning that you do is going to look pretty similar to what you can find with unsupervised machine learning. However, this option is going to spend time working on trial and error for how it solves problems instead. This can end up opening up a lot of opportunities that you may not be able to do when you work with a supervised or an unsupervised machine learning algorithms that we talked about earlier in this guidebook.

These are the basic types of reinforcement machine learning options that you can work with to make it easier to get the program to work the way that you would like. Take some time to work with each of these, and learn better how they are going to react to your program the way that it should behave overall.

Chapter 8: Top Applications of Working with Machine Learning

We have spent some time learning about what all machine learning is about, and how amazing it can be for some of the programmings that you want to work with. There are so many different things and applications that are going to use this coding, and as technology starts to become more advanced and changes in the future, more and more applications are likely going to be developed at the same time as well.

There are already a lot of applications that are going to be used regularly, along with machine learning.

Some of the most common ones are going to include options like image recognition, speech recognition, and predictions for many major companies when they are trying to sort through their data and know which way they should take their business in the future. With that in mind, let's explore a bit more about some of the top applications that you will be able to use with machine learning.

Image recognition

One of the most common applications of machine learning is that of image recognition. Most phones and many laptops are going to use this algorithm to help them recognize the faces of the users who are on them. There are a lot of situations where you may want the technology to classify a particular object and tell you what is in the image. The measurements of each digital image you want to pull up are going to give the user an idea of the output of each pixel in the image.

So, let's say that you want to look at an image that is all in black and white, the intensity that comes with all f the pixels that are in that image would help because they serve as the measurement. If the image ends up having M*M pixels, then we would denote this as having a measurement of M^2.

The cool thing is that when the machine has this kind of software put on it, it can go into the picture and split up the pixels so that you end up having three different measurements. These help you to know what the intensity level of the three primary colors, namely RBG, are. So, with the idea of M*M from before, then there are going to be three M^2 measurements.

Another part that comes with this is face detection. This is one of the most common categories that comes with image recognition software, and it is used to help detect whether the image has a face or not. There can also be a different category added, which allows you to make a new category for each person in your database.

You can also work with a part that is known as character recognition. When you add this to your machine learning program, you can segment out each piece of writing into the images of small sizes where each image contain one character. These categories are going to be comprised of the 26 letters of the English alphabet, as well as the first ten numbers and any special characters that come with it.

As you can see, there are already a lot of cool things that you can do when it comes to image recognition. It can help you to do security issues and recognition on some social media sites. Being able to recognize what is inside an image and developing more and more technology to help with this is something that we should expect in the future.

Speech recognition

Another thing that machine learning can help out with is the process of speech recognition. This is when an application can take spoken words, and either translates it back into some actual text or when it can follow a command of what you are telling it to do, including what we see with Amazon Echo and other similar products. Experts are going to refer to this application in a few different ways, including Computer Speech Recognition, Speech to Text, and Automatic Speech Recognition.

The programmer can use this to take spoken words and then trains the machineto recognize speech and to convert the words into text. Google and Facebook are two mainstream programs that are going to use this method to help train their machines. This works because the machines are going to use measurements to represent the signal of speech. These signals are going to be further then split up into distinct phenomes and words. The algorithm, if it is set up the right way, is going to use different energies to represent the signals that the speech sends out.

The details that you can see with this representation are going to be a bit more than what we will talk about in this book, but it is essential to know that all of the signals are going to relate to real signals. Applications out there that help with speech recognition will also to include an interface for the voice user, some of these including things like voice dialing and call routing on your phone. Depending on the application, these can use data entry and some of the other simple methods that are used to process information.

Prediction

Let's take some time to use our imagination here to think about how a bank works. In this scenario, a bank is going to try and calculate the probability of whether an applicant for a loan is going to pay for their loans or default on repayment. In order to help them calculate this risk probability, the system needs first to be able to identify, clean, and classify the data that is available in groups.

The analysts are going to classify the data based on certain criteria. Prediction is one of the most sought after uses of machine learning. And there are so many ways that it can be used. First, you will find many companies want to be able to use this in a way to help them to figure out whether or not they should take one action or another to help them to grow. This can help a bank figure out if one of their applicants is going to keep paying the loan. It can help retailers to figure out the best way to advertise their products to their customers, and it can help to figure out how sales will do in the future.

Anyone who has to do forecasts and make guesses about the way their business should go in the future is going to be able to benefit from this technology.

Instead of having to sift through all of the information on their own and hoping they get it right, or being new to the business and not having enough experience to back up the decisions, these business owners and decision makers can go in and use some of the algorithms of machine learning.

Machine learning, including a few of the algorithms that we talked about in this guidebook, are going to take a look at all of the information and data that you have. This could include information on customers, on their buying habits, on inventory, and past sales to name a few. It will then compute the information, and show the likely outcome, based on past events, that something is going to work for you or not. This makes it easier to know which decisions need to be made for your business.

Of course, these are not going to be accurate all of the time. There are going to be times when the predictions are going to be wrong, such as if there is a big change in the industry or the economy ends up going down. But they are going to be more accurate than what most humans can do on their own. And having someone who watches the market and prepares in case something drastic does change, and doing these predictions regularly will make a big difference.

Medical diagnosis

Machine learning is going to provide us with several methods, tools, and techniques that a doctor can use in their field to salve any diagnostic and prognostic problems at work. Doctors and patients can both use these techniques to enhance their medical knowledge and analyze the symptoms to figure out what the prognosis.

The results that you can get from this kind of analysis can be precious. You will find that it can open up the medical knowledge that most doctors have. Even skilled professionals are going to find there are certain conditions and treatments that they don't know about, and being able to work with machine learning can help them to do their job more efficiently. Doctors can use this machine learning to identify the irregularities in unstructured data, the interpretation of continuous data and to monitor results efficiently.

The use of this and how successful it is will help it to integrate computer-based systems with the healthcare environment and because this helps those in the medical world with a lot of opportunities to enhance and even improve the types of treatments they can provide.

When we are looking at medical diagnosis, the interest that comes with this is to establish the existence of the disease that is there, and then the doctor needs to work to identify the disease accurately. There are different categories for each disease that are under consideration, and then they can add in a category for a different disease that may not be present. Then, with the help of machine learning, it helps to improve the accuracy of diagnosis and analyzes the data of the patients. The measurements used are the results of the many medical tests conducted on the patient. The doctors are going to identify the disease using these measurements.

Statistical arbitrage

The next thing that you are going to be able to use machine learning is known as statistical arbitrage. This is a term that is going to be used in finance, so if you are working in this kind of field, it is going to be a good one to focus on. This will refer to the science of using trading strategies to help identify some of the short-term securities, which one can invest in.

When using these kinds of strategies, the user can implement in an algorithm on an array of securities based on the general economic variables and the historical correlation of the data. The type of measurement to use will help to resolve any problems that you have with estimation and classification. The assumption is that the stock price is going to always stay near its historical average overall.

Another strategy to focus on is the index arbitrage. This is going to be a strategy that is going to rely on the methods we have discussed with machine learning. The linear regression, as well as the support vector regression algorithms that we talked about before, are going to be so useful in helping the user calculate out the different prices that you will see with the funds and the stocks that you are interested in. And if you add in the principal component analysis, you will see that the algorithm breaks the data into various dimensions, which are used to identify the trading signals as a mean reverting process.

When it comes to investing, there are a lot of different parts that come into play, and being able to keep them organized and knowing how to use them with machine learning can take some practice. The buy, hold, sold, put, call or do nothing are just a few of the categories under which the algorithm places these securities under, based on what you want to do with it overall. The algorithm is then going to get to work helping you to calculate out the returns that you should expect in the future on each security. These estimates are going to help the user decide which security they want to buy and which security they would like to sell.

Learning associations

The final application that we are going to focus on when it comes to machine learning is known as the learning association. This is the process of trying to develop a good insight into the association between different groups of products that you have. There will be several products that are responsible for revealing this association, even if the two products or variables seem like they are completely unrelated. This kind of algorithm is useful because it takes into account the buying habits of the customers to figure out the best associations that are present.

One of these types of learning associations that can be used is known as basket learning analysis. This one, in particular, is going to deal with studying the association between products that were purchased by different customers. It is a type of application that works well at showing us how machine learning works.

With this one, we will assume that our Customer A bought product X. based on this purchase, we are going to use the options from machine learning to identify whether she is going to purchase product Y based on how these two products are associated together.

To make this easier, we can use the example of fish and chips to get the concept to work. If you have a new product that comes into the market, the association that was there between the previously existing products will also change. Sometimes it will change quite a bit, and sometimes the products are not related much to the new one, and their association is not going to change all that much. If one already knows the relationships between various products, they can go through and identify the right product to recommend to their customers.

And this is also one of the reasons that a lot of companies are happy to introduce their products in pairs, rather than individually. This helps them to promote two products, and make a bigger sale, by predicting the needs that their customer will have ahead of time and then meeting the need. If the customer sees two related products that go together and they are released at the same time, they are more likely to purchase both of these products together, knowing that they go together, and it increases the purchasing power and the capital for the company.

Big Data analysts are going to work with machine learning regularly to help them figure out what relationship is there when it comes to different products from the same company. The algorithms are going to be there and can often use the idea of probability and statistics, like we talked about earlier in this guidebook, to help come up with the relationship that is present in these products, and to help the company figure out which other products the customer is likely to purchase after they purchase the first one.

As you can see here, there are several different ways that machine learning can be used. And it can be used across a wide variety of different industries and in many ways. Whether it comes to using it to recommend products for a customer, you use it to make some predictions, or for some other reason, you will find that the things that machine learning is able to do already, and the applications that it is likely to be able to do in the future are already pretty amazing.

Chapter 9: Other Algorithms to Use in Machine Learning

In this guidebook, we have already talked about quite a few of the algorithms that you can use when it comes to working with machine learning. There are a lot of different ones that are available to make life a bit easier as well, but now, we are going to cover a few more of the ones that you may find useful if you are trying to progress some of your skills a bit more. Some of the other machine learning algorithms that you can use to help train any machine that you are using includes:

Dimension Reduction Methods

When we take a look at some of the databases that you may be using, it is possible that there could be millions or more records and variables that are there.

And you will need to use all of these variables to derive a good training data set. It is impossible to conclude that the variables are not going to be dependent on one another with any correlation between them. It is important for you to remember that there are often going to be more than one similarity between the variables. In this kind of situation, the predictor variable is going to be correlated in some way, and this is often going to have some kind of effect on the output.

Now, there are going to be times when there is a lot of instability arises in the solution set when there is multicollinearity between the variables leading to inconsistent results. For example, with this, if you are trying to look at more than one regression, there are multiple correlations between the predictor variables that have a significant impact on the output set.

However, individual predictor variables may not have a significant impact on the solution set. But, you may find that even when the programmer can identify a way to remove this instability (and they will often strive to make that happen), then there are going to be times when their user at some point may include variables with a high level of correlation between them. When this does happen, the algorithm will need to focus more on some parts of the input vector than to the others.

Now, you may have a data set that ends up with more than one kind of predictor variable, and when this happens, there is going to be a new complication that shows up. This complication is going to be where the algorithm must identify a model between the predictor and the variables that end up responding. This situation is going to complicate the analysis and its interpretation and violates the principle of parsimony.

So, what is this principle all about? This principle is going to state that as an analyst who is using machine learning, should always stick to a certain number of predictor variables, which makes it easy for human beings, as well as machines, to interpret the results. It is tempting to go through and retain a lot of different variables. But when this happens, there is going to be some possibility of a problem known as overfitting. You can try to do this, but it is likely going to hinder the analysis that you can get in the long run. Picking out one predictor to work with and getting everything else to fit with it is going to be the best.

The goal of working with this kind of method in machine learning is that we want to use the structure of correlation among the different variables of prediction. The reason that this is going to be done in this method is to help the programmer work towards the following goals:

1. Reduce the number of components for prediction in the set of data that you are using.

2. It can ensure that the components that you are using for predictions are going to be still independent of one another.

3. It can predict you with a dynamic framework, which is going to help in interpreting this kind of analysis.

There are a few methods that go under the idea of dimension reduction, and those are known as User Defined Composites and Factor Analysis and Principal Component Analysis.

Clustering

Another method that we need to take some time to explore here is known as clustering. This is going to be a technique of machine learning that can group different data points into a similar set of data. A programmer is often going to use this algorithm because it can take all of the points of data that they are using and will group them into groups that fit them the best.

The variables or the points of data that end up going into the same group need to be able to bear some similarities to one another. But the variables that are found in different groups shouldn't be alike at all. This needs to happen as much as possible. Clustering is known as one of the unsupervised machine learning algorithms, and it is often used when it is time to work with an analysis of a lot of statistical data.

Data scientists often like to use this kind of analysis of clustering to get some better insights into all of the data they have. If you have millions of points of data, it is hard to compute them all and understand what each one means and how it is going to be able to influence what you know and what you do with your points. But when you work with clustering, all of the information is going to be put into different groups (The number of groups will depend on how much data you have and how you can divide it up), and it will help you to read the information better than before.

There are going to be a few different types of clustering that you can work with depending on the kind of information that you need to cluster, how many categories you would like it split into, and more. Let's take a look at a few of these and see what they are all about and when you would use them.

K-Means

The K-Means clustering algorithm is one of the first to consider. This comes with the concept that every data scientist and engineer and anyone else who uses machine learning needs to know how to use it to get the right results. You need to learn more about this because it is easy to add to your code and will ensure you get your expected results. Some of the things that you will notice when it comes to the K-means algorithm include:

1. The algorithm is going to start the process by selecting the number of classes and the groups that you want to use. You will also need to come up with an idea of where the center points of these groups will be. If you are starting with a lot of data and you are not sure how many classes should be used, you can look through the data and see if you can get some ideas. You can also mess around with this a bit and experiment until you find the right number that seems to work for you.

2. The algorithm is then going to get to work trying to classify what the points of data are. It can do this by calculating the distance between the point and all of your center points. The programmer is then able to take a look at this distance and use it to categorize the data point in the class whose center is the closest to that point.

3. Using these classified points you just figured out, the algorithm is then going to compute where the center of the points is in the class by utilizing the mean here.

4. The programmer then needs to go through these steps a few times. It is going to continue doing this until the center of the groups does not change between the different iterations that you decide to do. You can also go through and try to initialize the centers in the groups

at random, and then select an iteration to give you the best results overall.

This is a clustering algorithm that you may need to use regularly. It has the advantage that it is so simple and fast to use, so it makes it easy to use as a beginner since you are going to use it to compute the distance between the variables and the center of the group. This works well because it gives you a good way to organize your information.

Of course, there are going to be a few disadvantages that are going to come with this option. First, you need to be able to accurately select the number of classes that you want to add into this simply by looking at the data. And if you have a ton of data, you may find that this is not ideal. And since you may want to find some insight about the data that you are using, it isn't ideal either. And since there are going to be some times when you will need to be random in how you select the center points that you use in the groups, this may cause you to come up with different results for each iteration.

If you want a method that is simple and easy to use and can help to separate your data points pretty well, then this method is going to be a great one that you should try out. With that said, there are going to be some times when you are not going to like working with this. You have to look at your data and figure out whether or not this is the right option for you.

Mean shift clustering

Another clustering is known as the mean shift clustering. This is going to be something that a programmer can use when they want to figure out and look through the dense areas that show up in their set of data. This algorithm is also useful because it will take a look at the center points of every group.

However, the main goal is that it can do some updates to some of the possible center points of the class within the sliding windows to locate the center point that you want. This can make it a bit better than the K-Means that we earlier talked about.

This mean shift clustering algorithm is going to remove the points that it chose for the center after it has gotten to the processing stage because this helps to reduce some of the duplicates that can sometimes form with these. And once it does this, the algorithm is going to move on to forming the final set of cluster points and placing them in their groups.

Let us first take a look at how this is going to look. Let us consider a set of points in a two-dimensional space. The first step that we need to take here is to define the point around which the circular sliding window is positioned. This window is going to have a radius of r called the kernel. This algorithm is going to be a hill-climbing algorithm, and it is constantly going to move the kernel to denser regions until the values can converge and come together.

Going back to this sliding window, it is going to continue to move to a denser region at every iteration. The algorithm can do this by shifting the center point of all the groups until you get the point that shows up at the mean. The density of the points in this window is going to be proportional to the number of data points found inside of it. So, if there are more points in this, this means that the density is going to be higher as well.

What this all means is that when you see a shift in the algorithm, it means that the mean of the point in the window is going to start moving over to the areas where the data seems to be denser than the other places.

This sliding window is going to keep on moving according to the change that shows up in the mean. The direction is not going to matter. It depends on where the mean ends up. The algorithm will then continue going through all of these steps, working with sliding windows that always change, until it can categorize all the points of data found in the set into different sliding windows.

If you do decide to use this method, you will not have to select the number of clusters or classes, which is one of the best advantages that come with this. It is also good that the center points are going to converge using a mean, and it moves to the mean that is found in the area that is the densest out of all of them. This is because this algorithm is going to understand the data, and it will try to fit it into any application that is driven by data. The selection of the kernel is not going to be as important with this one, but that, in some cases, is a major drawback that starts to occur.

If you are a beginner with the whole idea of machine learning and the clustering algorithms, then working with the K-means algorithm is going to be the best bet. But once you have a good understanding of how this method works and whether you will be able to use it for your needs or not, you will be able to try out the other algorithms for clustering to help make your analysis a bit better.

Working with regression modeling

Now that we have taken some time to explore what the world of clustering is all about in machine learning, it is time to move it a bit further and talk about regression modeling. This is an algorithm that is going to be used if the programmer would like to estimate the values of continuous target variables. There are going to be a variety of regression models that you can choose from, but one of the simplest forms is the linear regression model.

With the linear regression model, the algorithm will define the relationship between a continuous predictor variable and a continuous response variable using a straight line. There are going to be models that can use more than one of these variables for predicting things to define the response the variable.

Apart from the models that we already mentioned, there are going to be two other algorithms that can fit with this. These are called the logistic regression methods and the least squared regression. However, there are going to be some assumptions that come with these models, which can create some disparities. It is crucial that if you use this one a bit, you are going to need to validate the assumptions that you have before writing out the algorithm or even building the model.

If you have an engineer that will build up a model and use it without verifying the assumptions, then you have to be aware that you will get an output and you won't be able to use it since the model may have failed without the knowledge of the engineer.

When the programmer does get the result, they need to go through and check that there isn't going to be a linear relationship that shows up between the different variables of the models. There are going to be times when the set of data is going to have some variables that may be hidden with the linear relationship that they have. However, there is going to be a systematic approach that is there, known as inference, which the programmer can use to determine the linear relationship.

We need to take a look at some of the inference methods that the programmer can use to determine their relationship. Some of the best inference methods that you can use includes:

1. The t-test. This is going to be used to help you know the relationship between your two variables, the predictor and the response.

2. The confidence interval for the slope that shows up.

3. The confidence interval for the mean of the response variable given a value of the predictor.

4. The interval for the prediction that works for your random value of the response variable, given a value of the predictor.

The methods described above are going to often depend on the assumption that the programmer decides to make at the beginning of the process. It is easy for the programmer to assess whether the data can stick with the assumptions that you come with. You can check your assumptions with two main graphical methods. You will be able to do a plot of the standardized residuals and the plot of the normal probability.

A normal probability plot is going to be a quantile to quantile plot of the quantiles of distribution against the quantiles of a standard normal distribution to determine whether the distribution is going to deviate from what is seen as the normal or the mean. When you work with this plot, the programmer is going to make some comparisons between the value they observe for the distribution of interest, and compare it to the expected number of values that seem to occur with a distribution that is seen as normal.

If the programmer goes through and does this one, the bulk of the points in the plot should end up falling on or near a straight line. If there is a deviation from this plot, it is going to be seen as a deviation. A programmer is then able to validate their assumptions for the regression by seeing what patterns are going to show up on their plat. If they do notice a pattern is showing up, then the programmer can identify which assumptions don't seem to hold true well. However, if there isn't a pattern that shows up, then the assumptions can stay intact.

If you are taking a look through the graphs and they indicate that there is some violation of the assumptions you made, you may be able to apply a transformation to the response variable y, such as the ln (natural log or the log to the base of e) transformation. If the relationship between the response variables and the variables used for prediction, then the algorithm can be used for transformation.

Gaussian Mixture Models

The next thing is known as the Gaussian mixture models. These are a form of density estimation that you can use, and they will help give you an approximation of the probability distribution of your data. You are going to choose this model when you notice that your data is using multi-modal. This means there are going to be more than one bump or mode in the histogram. If you remember we talked about with probability, the mode is the most common.

So the Gaussian mixture will be the sum of the weighted Gaussians. To represent these weights, we're going to introduce a brand new symbol that we need to be called pi.

We are going to say pi(k) is the probability that your x value is going to belong to the kth Gaussian. Since pi(k) is a probability, there is going to be a constraint that all the pi's need to have a sum of 1. If this is confusing, another method that you can think of this is that we introduced a new latent variable that is called "z." "Z" is going to represent which Gaussian the data was coming from. So we can say pi(k) = P(z=k).

It is similar to saying that there is some hidden cause that is called "z" that we don't know about and we aren't able to measure from the beginning. But each of the "z"s is causing a new Gaussian to be generated, and we will be able to see that the data we place into the system is going to be the combined effects of those individual "z"s.

Training with the GMM is pretty similar to the k-means algorithm that we used earlier, which will make it a bit easier to learn. Two main steps will figure out the Gaussian, and they will be similar to what you use with the k-means.

The first step is to calculate the responsibilities. For this one, r(k,n) is going to be the responsibility of the kth Gaussian for generating the nth point. So, it's the proportion of that Gaussian, and then divide it by all of the Gaussians too. You can see that if pi(k) is larger here, then it is going to overtake the other Gaussians, and it should be about the value of 1. The algorithm that you would use for this one includes:

r(k,n) = pi(k)N(x(n), mu(k), C(k)) / sum[j=1..K]{pi(j)N(x(n), mu(j), C(j)) }

When working with the C(k), this is going to mean the covariance of the kth Gaussian. The N9x, mu, C) means the probability density function) of your Gaussian of the data point x and the mean mu and covariance C.

Once you have done this part, it is time to move on to step number two. This step will go through and recalculate all of the parameters of your Gaussians. This means the pi's, covariances, and the means. The method for going through and doing this is going to be pretty similar to what we did with the k-means, where we are going to weigh the influence of each sample on the parameter by using the responsibility. If the responsibility of the sample is small, this means that the "x" is going to matter less in the total of the calculation. Let's look at how we would go through and do this.

Define: $N(k)$ as $N(k) = \text{sum}[n=1..N]\{ r(k,n)\}$

Then each of the parameter updates will be the following:

$$mu(k) = sum[n=1..N]\{ r(k,n)x(n)] / N(k)$$

$$C(k) = sum[n=1..N]\{ r(k,n)(x(n) - mu(k))(x(n) - mu(k))\} / N(k)$$

$$pi(k) = N(k) / N$$

These are just a few of the different algorithms that you can use working with machine learning. As you read through this guidebook, you can start seeing a lot of options when working with machine learning. And often, it is going to depend on your purpose from the beginning. If you want to be able to look through and sort through all of the data you have, you may use one algorithm, but if you want to guess what products your past customers are going to use and purchase in the future, then the algorithm you use is going to be different.

And that is the beauty of working with machine learning. You will find that because there are already so many applications of working with machine learning, and it is likely going to continue growing throughout time, that these numerous learning behaviors are going to be necessary and one of them will come up in the future. Learning more about this process of how machine learning can make a difference in the coding that you can use.

Conclusion

Thank for making it through to the end of *Machine Learning*. Let's hope it was informative and able to provide you with all of the tools you need to achieve your goals whatever they may be.

The next step is to get started with some of the building blocks, information, and algorithms that we talked about in this guidebook.

There is so much to love when it comes to working with machine learning, and many people are starting and have no idea what all of this even means.

This guidebook is meant to help you to get started, to gain a better understanding of what machine learning is all about, and even how to start using it in your business or on some of your projects.

This guidebook took some time to discuss more machine learning and all of the cool things that you can do with it. You will enjoy that it can help to sort through large amounts of data (which is useful for any business who wants to plan out for the future in the most efficient manner), works with search engines, voice recognition and so much more. If you can imagine a project that you want to do, but you worry that traditional coding languages are going to struggle with it, then this guidebook and the machine learning techniques that are inside will be the right option for you.

From there, we spent some time bringing it all together and exploring some of the cool things you can do when working with machine learning.

We talked about how it compares to artificial intelligence, some of the basic building blocks and some examples that you need to know when getting started, and then we moved on to some of the best algorithms that you can use, based on the situation and the project on hand. When you put all of this information together, you will be able to find plenty of uses for machine learning, and how to make it work for you.

There are so many neat things that you can do with machine learning. Many programmers, whether they are well-versed in some of the old traditional ways of coding or they are new to the arena, have found that working with machine learning can make things easier and opens up many doors of opportunities. When you are ready to learn a bit more about machine learning and how to use it for your business or some of your projects, make sure to check out this guidebook to help you get going!

Python Machine Learning

Everything You Should Know About Python Machine Learning Including Scikit Learn, Numpy, PyTorch, Keras And Tensorflow With Step-By-Step Examples And PRACTICAL Exercises

JOSEPH MINING

Introduction

The following chapters will discuss all the different parts of machine learning that you can do using the Python coding language. When these two programming ideas come together, there are so many things that you can do, and the applications are endless! This guidebook will discuss the basics of Python machine learning, and how you can get started—even as a beginner.

To start this guidebook, we shall consider the basics of machine learning and then move on to some of the basic parts of working with Python when you combine it with machine learning. Therefore, if you have never worked in coding, or at least, have never done any work with the Python coding language, we also have a chapter that will explore a few of the basics that you need to know to start writing your Python codes. Also, how to set up the right environment with the right libraries, so that you can get started with writing codes for machine learning.

From here, we are going to take a look at Scikit-Learn and this library and its importance before moving on to some of the different algorithms that you can work within machine learning using Python coding language. Some of the algorithms that we will explore here will include the KNN, K-

Means Clustering, Support Vector Machines, Neural Networks, Random Forests, Recurrent Neural Networks, and Linear Classifiers. We can then end the guidebook with a brief talk about some other amazing things you can do with Python machine learning, and how much it can help you with your programming goals.

Many people are interested in learning more about machine learning, and in using the Python coding language to help them see the best results. When you are ready to see what machine learning is all about, as well as how you can combine it with your codes and applications to get the best results, then make sure to read through this guidebook to help you get started!

There are plenty of books on this subject on the market—thanks again for choosing this one! Every effort was made to ensure it is full of as much useful information as possible. Please enjoy!

Chapter 1: Understanding the Basics of Machine Learning

The first thing to explore in this guidebook is some of the basics that come with machine learning. It isn't going to do us much good to learn the Python code and the different parts that come with that, as well as how to use it with machine learning if we have no idea what machine learning is all about. Machine learning is sometimes known as a form of artificial intelligence that provides a computer or another system with the ability to learn from its own past experiences, rather than it being programmed ahead of time with everything that it should know how to do. This makes it more versatile and better at its job overall and opens up so many doors and opportunities that aren't present with traditional coding.

This learning process can begin with some data or observations—like instructions for the code, examples, and even direct experiences so that the machine can find the right patterns from that data. Then, the machine can take those predictions to know what it can do in the future. The main goal with machine learning here is that it will allow a computer to learn on its own automatically without someone coming in and adjusting things, or having to code out for every situation.

Any time that machine learning shows up in your process, you may find that it will make analyzing information, especially larger amounts of data, really easy. Machine learning can even give you some of the most profitable results—but before you can get to that point, you need to have a good understanding of what it takes to make all this happen.

While there are many uses and advantages to machine learning, it is coding that will take a bit more work than others. This is because you are working on training the models of machine learning how to behave and learn, even when you are not there to show it how to behave. This is a bit more difficult to code, but it is going to do wonders when it comes to increasing the number of things the system can do.

There are different things that you can use the processes of machine learning. If you are uncertain about how the input will be from the user, or if you aren't sure how the result will be, then machine learning can be useful. If you would like the computer to sort through the data and come up with some predictions for you, then machine learning can be helpful as well. Some good examples of what you can use machine learning for include:

1. Voice recognition

2. Facial recognition

3. Search engines – The machine learning program is going to start learning from the answers that the individual provides, or the queries, and will start to give better answers near the top as time goes on.

4. Recommendations after shopping

5. Going through large amounts of data about finances and customers and making accurate predictions about what the company should do to increase profits and happy customers along the way

These are a few examples that you may find useful in figuring out what machine learning can do. It is likely that over time, the applications of this are going to grow as more programmers learn how to use it for their needs. Many of the traditional programs that you have learned are going to be much simpler than this, but this means that they are going to be a bit limited on what they can do. You have to tell the system exactly what it is allowed to do or not do. And this doesn't allow for a lot of different options from the user along the way.

This coding is not always going to be the best option, especially with some of the examples that we are going to show you with machine learning. For example, if you are trying to put together a search engine, it is impossible to figure out all the different search queries that the user will put into it. Or, if you are working with some of the voice recognition software that is out there, it is impossible to figure out ahead of time each request, or how each person is going to talk. These are things you would need to know with traditional coding, making it impossible to use. But machine learning can handle it.

The Importance of Bringing Python On Board

While we are going to take a closer look at the Python coding language and how it works in a bit, it is essential to note here that we are using Python with machine learning because it is one of the best languages for doing this. Python coding is simple, making it easy enough for a beginner to start with, but it still has plenty of power behind it to ensure that you are going to get the work done. The Python language also comes with a big library, it can work well with other languages if you need to have two or more work together, and it is easy to read, even as a beginner.

As we go through this guidebook, you will notice that a lot of the examples that we take a look at are going to be in Python.

This is going to help you learn a bit about the Python language while also seeing how some of the machine learning algorithms work.

There are a lot of other coding languages that can work well with machine learning. But often, they add a layer of complications to the process, and they are often saved for those who know that particular language well or some of the most sophisticated options with machine learning.

The Python language is so much better at helping you to complete your tasks. It is simple to work with, easy to understand, and does have all the power you need to work with the algorithms in this guidebook. We will even go through some of the algorithms and show you the different Python codes that you can use to get the most out of each one. There is nothing like the ease of use, power, and variety that you can find when you use the Python coding language, even when it comes to machine learning.

Classifying Algorithms in Machine Learning

Another thing that we need to note here is that there are a few types of algorithms that go with machine learning—three, to be exact. These include reinforced learning, unsupervised learning, and supervised learning.

Supervised Learning

First on the list is supervised learning. This one is going to involve the help of a person the most out of the three. A computer programmer is going to need to provide the computer with some input and tell it the desired output— meaning that they need to furnish the right feedback to the system based on how accurate the predictions of the system are during that training session. This is going to mean that the trainer will need to show the system a lot of examples, and show what answers are right and what aren't, which allows the system to learn along the way.

After the training, the algorithm is then going to take the knowledge that it learned from the data and then works to make the best predictions. The concept of this learning is similar to learning in a classroom. The teacher will hand out a lesson to the students, usually providing some examples. And from this, the students can derive the new rules and the knowledge that they need to gain from these examples. The students can then take that knowledge and apply it to different situations, even if the new data isn't the same as the information they got during training.

Any time that we are looking towards this learning, it is good to note that there are going to be some differences that show up between regression problems and classification problems. A regression problem to start with is going to be when the target is a numeric value of some kind. But the classification means that it will have a tag or a class.

A regression task can sometimes help the programmer figure out the average of the cost of all the houses for sale in town, for example. And then the classification problem would help you figure out what flower is inside a picture that is given, based on the petal length and other factors.

Supervised learning is what will occur at any time that you choose an algorithm that can learn the right response to the data at hand based on what the user gives to it. There are different methods that machine learning of this kind can do. It can look at the examples and some other targeted responses that you can provide to the computer. The program is also able to look at examples and some other targeted responses that are given to the computer even in the form of values and strings so that it can learn the right way to behave.

Supervised learning is a pretty simple process to work with. You are going to show the system a lot of different examples of what is right, and from that, it can look at new examples and determine if they match up and are right, or if they don't match up and would be considered wrong.

Unsupervised Learning

Another form of machine learning that you can work with is known as unsupervised machine learning. With these kinds of algorithms, you do not have to go through and provide the data to the computer like we had to do above. This is because you would rather have the machine learn what the output should be based on an unknown input. An approach that is called deep learning, or the iterative approach is going to be used to review the data and help you come up with new conclusions.

What ends up making the unsupervised learning approach more suitable for a lot of different processing tasks, which are going to be more complicated to deal with. This allows the learning algorithms to learn from examples, without a response to it. The algorithm is going to strive to find the right patterns that come from these examples all on its own rather than having the programmer tell it the answers.

Many of the recommended systems that you encounter, such as when you are purchasing something online, are going to work with the help of an unsupervised learning algorithm. In this case, the algorithm is going to derive what to suggest to purchase based on what you went through and purchased before. The algorithm then has to estimate the customers you resemble the most based on your purchases and then provide you with some good recommendations from there.

As we mentioned a little bit before, there is more than one machine learning that you can work with. Supervised learning is the first one. It is designed for you to show examples to the computer, and then you teach it how to respond based on the examples that you showed. There are a lot of programs where this technique is going to work well, but the idea of showing thousands of examples to your computer can seem tedious. Plus, there are many programs where this is not going to work all that well.

And this is where you are going to notice that machine learning is going to be useful. Unsupervised learning allows the system to learn either from the given examples or from mistakes without a response that goes with either of them. This means that with the unsupervised algorithms, they are going to be in charge of figuring out and also analyzing the data patterns based on the given input.

There are a few options that you can choose from when you want to do an algorithm of unsupervised machine learning. No matter which algorithm you decide to use, it is going to take the data that you provide, and can then restructure it so that all of the data ends up in some classes. This makes it easier for anyone, even if they are not a programmer to take a look at the information and form some conclusions from it. And unsupervised machine learning is going to be the best one to get this done.

Reinforcement Learning

And the third machine learning to consider is the idea of reinforcement learning. This happens when the algorithm is presented with some examples that don't come with labels, pretty similar to what we see with unsupervised learning. However, with this learning type, there is going to be negative and positive feedback based on the solution that the algorithm suggests. The applications that will tend to use this needs to decide on its own, and then these decisions will either be right or wrong with consequences to match. Think of this learning as trial and error.

Errors are fine with this method because they ensure that the model is better with learning and making predictions later on. The learning method is going to have some penalty—such as pain, cost, or a loss in time if they get the answer wrong. This helps to learn what to avoid and will direct it to the path of making the right decision.

You will find that the learning processes that come with machine learning will be similar to what is seen with data mining and predictive modeling. In both of these scenarios, these patterns can be adjusted inside the program accordingly—a good example of how this may work with the system for recommendations. If you decide to purchase an item online, if the site has this, then you will see an ad that is going to be related to that item.

Some programmers will think that unsupervised learning and reinforcement learning is the same thing. There are some similarities with it, but there are differences. First, the input given in these algorithms will need to have some mechanisms for feedback. You can set them up to be positive or negative, and this is going to depend on the algorithm that you choose to work with.

Any time you want to work with this machine learning, you will see that this is going to work like trial and error. Think about when you are working with a younger child. When they end up going through and doing an activity that you didn't approve, you will start by telling them it is time to stop, or you will do another consequence that you thought through ahead of time. Then, there will be times when the child will do actions that you approve of, and you will need to take some time to praise them and let them know they are doing the right things. With these two steps, the child will start to learn acceptable behavior.

This is the same idea that reinforcement learning is going to work with as well. This whole process is going to work on the idea of trial and error, and it will require that your application uses an algorithm to help it make the right decisions. It is a good one to use if you want an algorithm to make decisions without any mistakes and a good outcome. Remember that your program is going to need some time to learn. It is going to make some mistakes along the way, but as it does this trial and error more often, it is going to get better at doing the work.

Understanding What Deep Learning Is About

The next thing is the idea of deep learning. This is going to be a subfield of machine learning involving algorithms that are inspired by the function and structure of the brain known as artificial neural networks. It is going to work to teach your computer to act and behave the way that is natural to humans, that is, that the system will be able to learn by example.

It is through the help of this deep learning that your computer is going to learn how to perform the various classification tasks directly from sound, image, and text. Deep learning models can achieve state-of-the-art accuracy, which in some cases, will be able to exceed the performance that you can get at the human level. Large sets of labeled data and neural network architectures are going to be used to train models with some deep learning.

As you can see, there are a lot of different parts that can come with machine learning. It is a great tool that you can use to get your computer or your system to do some of the things that you may struggle with. For example, machine learning can be used to help work with search engines, and maybe provide you with some recommendations when you are shopping online. Even if you need to sort through a large amount of data, machine learning can come into play and help out.

The rest of this guidebook will discuss some of the basics that come with machine learning, and how to work with it on Python, to ensure that you can get the most out of this process. Let's take a closer look at some of the processes that you need to know to see amazing results with machine learning with Python.

Chapter 2: Some of the Basic Parts of Working with Python and Machine Learning

Now that we have a better understanding of what machine learning is all about, it is time to move on to some more of the things that you will be able to do with machine learning and how two of the libraries from Python are going to come in and help you make the process easier. You will notice that both of these work well with Python, and they are there to ensure that the codes you write in Python will be as effective and strong as possible. And since they can work with machine learning, you are going to enjoy the benefits as well.

The two main processes and libraries that we need to look at in this chapter will include TensorFlow and Scikit-Learn. Let's explore more about what these are like, and why they can be so crucial to your program on a machine learning project.

What Is Scikit-Learn?

We also need to take some time to learn about Scikit-learn. This is going to provide your users with several supervised and unsupervised learning algorithms through a consistent Python interface. We are going to learn more about Python later in this guidebook, but it is a fantastic tool that you can use to enhance your machine learning, and since it is for beginners, even those who have never worked with coding in the past will be able to use it.

David Cournapeau in 2007 as a Google Summer of code project developed the Scikit-learn. This process is going to be suitable to use whether you need it commercially or academically.

Scikit-learn has been in use as a machine learning library inside of Python. It is going to come with numerous classification, regression, and clustering to help you get more results. Some of the algorithms that you will get to use with this system is going to include DBSCAN, k-means, random forests, support vector machines, and gradient boosting, to name a few. And Scikit-learn was designed so that it would work well with some of the other popular libraries found on the Python code, including with SciPy and Numpy libraries.

This particular library, in particular, has been all done by Python, but some of the different formulas and algorithms that you are going to rely on to make this one work will be written with the help of Cython. If you want to make sure that the performance that you get is the best with this, you will find that the Scikit-Learn library is the one that you need to focus on. It is, especially good at building up some of the models that you need with machine learning. And since it is an open-sourced library, and easy to get started with, you will easily be able to open it up and start using it as soon as needed.

Understanding More About Tensor Flow

The second topic that we are going to explore in this chapter is a second library known as TensorFlow. This is a framework that you can get through the Google platform, and it is used when you want to create some models in deep learning. This TensorFlow library is often going to rely on some data flow graphs that work on numerical computations. And it can stop in and make the process of machine learning easier than before.

You will find that working with TensorFlow makes the process of getting data, of training the models that you would like to use with machine learning, of making predictions, and even modifying some of the results that you see in the future so much easier. Since all of these are going to be important when it comes to machine learning, you can see why we want to spend some time learning TensorFlow.

TensorFlow is a library that the Brain team from Google developed to use on machine learning, and it is especially effective when you want to do some machine learning on a larger scale. TensorFlow is going to bring together algorithms that work with deep learning and machine learning, and it helps to make them more useful trough a common metaphor.

Just like what we saw when we were working on the other library, TensorFlow is going to work together well with Python, and it will ensure that you can have a front-end API that can be used when you would like to build a new application. And when you execute these applications, you will see them done in what is known as high-performance C++.

TensorFlow can be used to help out with running deep neural networks, for training, building, handwritten digit classifications, recurrent neural networks, word embedding, and even natural language processing to name a few of the neat things you will be able to do.

Both of these two libraries work well with Python, and they are going to do a remarkable job when it comes to ensuring that you are on the right track with your machine learning. Both of these are going to take on a lot of different tasks, and you will need to pick out the right one based on what you would like to get done on your project.

Chapter 3: What Is Python, and How Do I Use It?

We have spent some time talking about the Python coding language and some of the neat things that you can do with this. However, to complete this book, we also need to get a good understanding of the Python language and what it is all about. Different parts show up in the Python coding language, but knowing some of the basics, as well as, learning some of the power that comes with Python makes all of the difference on the success that you can get when you combine this coding language with machine learning.

We have talked briefly about the Python coding language already, as well as some of the reasons why it may be so beneficial when you want to work with machine learning. Even though it is considered one of the easier coding languages to learn how to work with, it has a lot of power and strength that comes in behind it, which makes it the best option to use whether you are a beginner or someone who has been coding for quite some time. And since the Python language does have some of the power of the bigger and more powerful coding languages, you will be able to do a lot of cool things with machine learning.

There are going to be a few different parts that come into play when you start to learn how to work with the Python code even with machine learning. You can work with the comments, functions, statements, and more. Let's take a look at some of the basic parts that come with coding in Python so that we can do some of these more complicated things together as we progress through machine learning.

The Comments

The first aspect of the Python coding language that we need to explore is that of comments. There is going to be some point when you are writing out a code where you would like to take a break and explain to others and yourself what took place in the code. This is going to ensure that anyone who sees the code knows what is going on at one point to another. Working with a comment is the way that you would showcase this in your project, and can make it easier for others to know the name of that part, or why you are doing one thing compared to another.

When you would like to add in some comments to the code, you are going to have a unique character that goes in front of your chosen words. This unique code is going to be there to help you tell the computer program that it should skip reading those words and move on to the next part of the code instead.

The unique character that you are going to use for this one is the # sign in front of the comments you are writing. When the compiler sees this, it is going to know that you don't want that part of the code to execute at all. It will wait until the next line before it gets started with rereading the code. An example of a comment that you may see in your code would include:

```
#this is a new comment. Please do not execute in the code.
```

After you have written out the comment that you want here, and you are done with it, you are then able to hit the return button or enter so that you can write more code that the compiler can execute. You can have the freedom to comment as long or as short as you would like based on what you would need in the code. And you can write in as many of these comments as you would like. It is usually seen as a better option if you keep the comments down to what you need. Otherwise, it makes the code start to look a little bit messy overall. But you can technically add in as many of these comments to your code as you would like.

The Statements

The next part of the code that we need to focus on is the statements. Any time that you are starting with your new code, whether you are working with Python or with some other coding language along the way, you must add these statements inside of the code. This allows the compiler to know what you would like to happen inside. A statement is going to be a unit of code that you would like to send to your interpreter. From there, the interpreter is going to look over the statement and execute it based on the command that you added in.

Any time you decide to write out the code, you can choose how many statements are needed to get the code to work for you. Sometimes, you need to work with one statement in a block of code, and other times, you will want to have more than one. As long as you can remember that the statements should be kept in the brackets of your code, it is fine to make the statement as long as you would like, and include as many statements as you would like.

When you are ready to write your code and add in at least one statement to your code, you would then need to send it over so that the interpreter can handle it all. As long as the interpreter can understand the statements that you are trying to write out, it is going to execute your command. The results of that statement are going to show up on the screen. If you notice that you write out your code and something doesn't seem to show up in it the right way, then you need to go back through the code and check whether they are written the right way or not.

Now, this all may sound like a lot of information, but there is a way to minimize the confusion and ensure that it can make more sense to you. Let's take a look at some examples of how this is all going to work for you.

```
x = 56

Name = John Doe

z = 10


print(x)

print(Name)

print(z)
```

When you send this over to the interpreter, the results that should show up on the screen are:

```
56

John Doe

10
```

It is as simple as that. Open up Python, and give it a try to see how easy it is to get a few things to show up in your interpreter.

The Variables

The next things we consider inside our Python codes are the variables. These variables are important to learn about because they are the part that will store your code in the right places so you can pull them up later on. This means that if you do this process in the right way, the variables are going to be found inside the right spot of the memory in the computer. The data in the code will help determine which spots of the memory these points will be stored on, but this makes it easier for you to find the information when it is time to run the code.

The first thing that we need to focus on here is to make sure that the variable has a value assigned to it. If there is a variable without a value, then the variable won't have anything to save and store. If the variable is given a good value from the start, then it will behave the way you are expecting when you execute the program.

When it comes to your Python code, there are going to be three types of variables that you can choose from. They are all important and will have their place to work. But you have to choose the right one based on the value that you would like to attach to that variable. The main variables that are available for you with Python are going to include:

1. Float: This is going to be an integer variable that includes numbers like 3.14

2. String: This is going to be one of those statements that you would write out. You can add in any phrase that you would like to this one.

3. Whole number: This is going to be any of the other numbers that you would want to use, ones that are not going to contain a decimal.

When you are trying to work with the variables in your program, you won't have to go through and make a declaration to make sure the memory space is available. This is something that Python can do for you automatically, as soon as a value is assigned to a variable. If you would like to make sure that this is happening in your code and avoid some of the surprises along the way, you need to double check that the equal sign, the sign of giving a variable value is in the right place. An excellent example of how this is going to look when you write out a code includes the following

```
x = 12              #this  is  an  example  of  an  integer
assignment

pi = 3.14           #this  is  an  example  of  a  floating
point assignment

customer  name  =  John  Doe  #this  is  an  example  of  a
string assignment
```

In some instances, you may need to have one variable with two or more values attached to it. There are certain times when you won't be able to avoid this and need to make it happen. The good news is that you can work with the same procedure discussed above to make this happen, you need to make sure that there is an equal sign to each part so that the compiler knows how to assign everything. So, when you want to do this, you would want to write out something like a = b = c = 1.

The Keywords

Any time that you are using the Python language, like what we find in other coding languages as well, you are going to come across some words that are reserved as commands in the code, and these are going to be known as keywords. You need to be careful about the way you use these because they are there to tell the program some commands, and how you would like it to behave. You don't want to bring these and use them in any other place outside of a particular command.

If you do misuse these keywords, it is going to cause some confusion inside the code. The interpreter isn't going to know what to do, and the computer may get stalled in what it needs to do. As we go through this guidebook some more and develop a few Python codes for machine learning, we will start to recognize some of the most common keywords that you need to watch out for.

Naming Your Identifiers

The next thing that we need to focus on is how to name all of the identifiers. You need to do this in a way that makes sense, and will not confuse the computer along the way. Any time that you are writing out a particular code in Python, you are going to have at least a few identifiers that show up. Some of the most common of these identifiers are going to including classes, entities, variables, and functions.

At one point or another, you will need to name out the identifiers so that they are more likely to work in the way that they should and make it easier for the compiler to pull them up when it is time to execute the code. No matter which of the four identifiers that you use, the rules for naming are going to be the same, which can make it easier when you get started. Some of the rules you should remember when naming your identifiers include:

Any time that you are using letters, it is fine to use either upper case or lower case, and a combination of both is fine as well. You can also add in numbers, symbols, and an underscore to the name. Any combination of these are acceptable, make sure that there are no spaces between the characters of the name.

Never start the name of one of your identifiers with a number. This means that writing out the name of 4babies would result in an error on your computer. However, it is acceptable to name an identifier `fourbabies` if you would like.

The identifier should never be one of the Python keywords, and the keyword should not appear in the name at all.

Now, if you are trying to go through and write out a few of your codes along the way, and you don't follow all of the rules that are above, you will confuse the compiler, and it will send you an error message to let you know something is wrong. The error will then be on your computer, and the program will close out because it doesn't know how to proceed. This is something that you don't want to happen, so be careful when naming these identifiers.

Another thing to remember with these identifiers and naming them is that you want to make sure that you are picking out names that are ready for you to remember. And picking out names that are easy to understand and read will make it easier if another programmer comes in, and is trying to look through the code as well.

What Else Do I Need to Know About the Python Coding Language?

The Python coding language is often considered to be one of the best languages for programming by the experts, and this is even truer if you are someone who has never worked with coding in the past. This language is simple, it has plenty of power, and there are a lot of the tools and the resources that are needed to help you work on your project, even if that project has to do with machine learning. While there are other options that you can use with machine learning, those are often a bit more difficult to work with, and Python is often the better choice.

One thing that you will like when you first start working with the Python language is that the whole thing is based on the English language. What this means is that you will recognize the words and what they mean, rather than trying to guess. And even though it is a language that is great for beginners who have never worked with coding before, it is going to be strong enough to work with machine learning and any other topic that you would like.

As someone ready to learn and get started with the Python language, you will notice that it has a nice big library available that you can utilize when you are coding. And this library is going to have the tools and the resources that you need, making it easier for beginners and experts alike to write out any code that they need.

Chapter 4: How to Set Up the Perfect Environment in Python

The next thing that we need to work on here is to set up your environment to start with machine learning and see the results that you want. Now that we know a bit more about how all of this works with machine learning and a bit about the Python coding language, it is time to set up the environment so that you can get started. This is a crucial step to take before you try to start on any machine learning and deep learning techniques. And to help you get all of this setup, you need to make sure that your two libraries—Scikit-Learn and TensorFlow—are all set up and ready to get started.

Getting Started with Scikit-Learn

Both the Scikit-Learn and the TensorFlow library are going to need to be set up to start with Python machine learning. But the first one that we are going to work with setting up is the Scikit-Learn. This is a library that you can work with if you have Python 2.7 or higher on your system. If those are installed already, then you should already have things set up here. It is usually best if you are working with machine learning that you have one of these newer versions, so installing that can help.

Before you start with installing this library, double check and see if the SciPy and Numpy libraries are installed already —if these are not present, then you need to install them first, and then go through and install the Scikit-Learn.

The installation of these libraries may seem like it is time-consuming; it is essential and can do this with the help of pip. This pip is going to be a tool that will come along with Python, so can use the pip as soon as the system is all installed. From here, you can work with the command below to help you get the Scikit-Learn library ready to go:

From here, the installation will be able to run, and then it will complete once all of that is done. It is also possible for you to go through and use the option of `conda` to help install this library. The command that you will want to use to make sure that this happens is:

```
conda install scikit-learn
```

Once you notice that the installation of scikit-learn is complete, it is time to do some importation to get it over to the Python program. This step is necessary to use the algorithms that come with it. The good news is that the command to make this happen is going to be done. You need to go to your command line and type in import `sklearn`.

If your command can go through without leaving behind an error message, then you know that the installation that you did was successful. After you are done with all of these steps, your scikit-learn library is on the computer, it is compatible with the Python program, and it is going to be ready to use.

Installing TensorFlow

Once you have the Scikit-Learn library put in place on your environment, it is time to start installing the TensorFlow library. When you download this one, you can get a few different APIs for other programming languages outside Python, including Java and C++, so if you need to use these, you can get a hold of them pretty easily. You can download this on a few different devices if you would like, but for this guidebook, we are going to discuss how you can install this library on a Windows computer. You can use the pip that we had from before, or Anaconda, to get this downloaded on your Windows computer.

The native pip is often the best way to get TensorFlow installed on your system, without having to worry about the virtual environment that comes with it. But one of the things that you are going to need to keep track of here is that when you install this library with a pip, there are times when this will interfere with some of the other installations of Python that are on the computer, and you need to be aware of this ahead of time.

The good thing to know here is that the only thing that you need to have up and running to make this work is a single command. And once you know this command, TensorFlow can install on your system and get it up and running. Once you can get this library installed using the pip, the user is going to see that there are some options, including the ability to choose which directory you would like to store this on.

Now, you can also choose to install the TensorFlow library on your computer with the help of Anaconda. To do this, you need first to go through and create your virtual environment. You may also want to work with a pip with this one as well. Before you start on this one, make sure that you have a Windows system and Python 3.5 or above. Pip 3 program needs to be in place as well to help with this kind of installation. The commands you will need to get started with this one include:

```
pip3 install - upgrade tensorflow
```

If you would like to install the GPU version of the Tensorflow program, you would need to go through and use the following command to make it happen:

```
pip3 install - upgrade tensorflow-gpu
```

This is going to ensure that you install TensorFlow on the Windows system that you are using. But another option is to install this library so that you can use it with Python and all of your other machine learning algorithms will include being able to install it with the help of the Anaconda package.

Pip is a program that is automatically going to get installed when you get Python on your system. But the Anaconda program isn't. This means that if you would like to make sure that TensorFlow is installed with the use of the Anaconda program, you first need to take the time to install this program. To do this, visit the website for Anaconda, download it from the website, and then find the instructions for installation from that same site.

Once you have gone through and installed the Anaconda program, you should notice that it comes with a package that is called conda. This is a good package to take some time to look at and explore a bit because it will work when you want to manage any installation packages or manage virtual environments. To get some access to this package, you need to start up the Anaconda program.

After you get to this point, you can head over to the Windows main screen and then click on the Start menu. You can choose All Programs and expand it out until you see the folder for Anaconda. You click on this prompt to launch the folder. If you need to see what details are in this package, you can run a command in the command line for "conda info." This makes it easier to see what the details for that package and the manager as well.

There are a lot of cool things that come with this Anaconda program, but one of the options that you will want to learn more about to help with machine learning. Anaconda can help you create an environment of Python for your own using this package. The virtual environment is going to be its isolated copy of Python, and it will have the right capabilities of maintaining all of the files that it needs, including the directories and paths. This can be helpful because it allows you to do all of these things while still working with the version of Python that you want and any of the other libraries that you want.

These virtual environments may seem like they are complicated, but it is helpful because they will provide you with a way to isolate your projects, and can avoid some of the significant problems that can arise along the way. Note that this is going to be a separate environment compared to the normal Python environment that was downloaded before. This is important because you won't be able to have any effect on the regular Python environment, whether it is bad or good.

At this point, we want to do some work to help us create a virtual environment for that TensorFlow package. This can be done when we use the command of "conda create." Since we want to create a brand new environment that we have called `tensorenviron`, we would need to use the formula below to help:

```
conda create -n tensorenviron
```

At this point, the program is going to ask you whether or not you would like to allow the process of creating the environment to continue, or if you would like to cancel the work. You will want to type in the "y," and then hit the enter key to move on. This will allow the installation to continue successfully to see the results that you want.

Once you have been able to go through this whole thing and create an environment, you will need to take a few minutes and let this environment activate it. If you do not do the activation correctly, you won't be able to use this new environment—you won't be able to get the new environment to work, either. You will be able to activate this using the command discussed earlier. From that point, you will then be able to list out the name that you would like for the environment. An excellent example of what we are talking about here and how it will work includes:

```
Activate tensorenviron
```

Now that you have been able to activate the TensorFlow environment, it is time to go ahead and make sure that the package for TensorFlow is going to be installed, too. You can do this by using the command below:

```
Conda install tensorflow
```

From here, the computer is going to present you with a list of all of the different packages that you can install together along with the package for TensorFlow if you would like. You will be prompted to decide if you want to install these packages or not. You can then type in the "y," and hit the enter key on the keyboard.

Once you agree to do this, the installation of this package is going to get started right away. However, notice that this particular process for installation is going to take a bit of time, so you need to wait and remain patient. However, the speed of your connection will determine the amount of time that the installation process is going to take. The progress and how far the installation has gone and yet to go will be shown on a prompt window.

After a certain time, the installation process is going to be complete, and you can then determine if the installation process was successful or not. This is pretty easy to do because you need to run the import statement with Python. The statement is going to be done from the regular terminal of Python. If you are doing this with the Anaconda prompt, you can type in "python" and hit the enter key. This is going to make sure that you end up in the terminal for Python, and from there, you can run the import statement below:

```
Import tensorflow as tf
```

If you find that the package wasn't installed properly, you are going to end up with an error message on the screen after you do this code. If you don't see an error message, then you know that the installation of the package was successful.

Chapter 5: What Is Scikit-Learn, and Why Should I Learn About It?

There are a lot of things that you are going to enjoy when it comes to the Scikit-Learn environment and library. This is one of the best options that you can work with through Python and will make your machine learning projects so much more successful than before. If you are a programmer who is learning how to work with the process of machine learning, or you want to do more with your Python codes, then you need to make sure you have a good understanding of this library and how it works.

The Scikit-Learn library was developed in 2007. Later, the company started growning and made a lot of changes over time. Currently, it gets to enjoy more than 30 active contributors, and there are even some paid sponsorships from the INRIA, Google, and the Python Software Foundation to ensure that this library is going to be developed. And it is all done in a way that ensures that the user is not going to have to pay   to   use   it!

But this starts to bring up some questions about this library, and what it is all about. This library is going to ensure that the computer programmer has a lot of algorithms for both the unsupervised learning and the supervised learning that they want to do. And these algorithms are adjusted so that they can stay consistent with the Python environment. This means that you can use these algorithms and work on some machine learning projects all on Python.

This particular library is going to be licensed under what is known as a permissive simplified BSD license, and many of the Linux distributions can use it as well. It will be built using the SciPy library that will help make things even easier. The stack that is found inside of this, and which you will find helpful when you are working with machine learning includes:

1. NumPy: This is a good one to use because it allows you to work on the n-dimensional array package

2. SciPy: This one is going to be a fundamental library to use if you wish to do computations in the scientific field

3. Matplotlib: This is a good library to use because it helps you do some plotting, whether in 2D or 3D.

4. iPython: This is a good library to use because it is going to allow you a console that is more enhanced and interactive than others.

5. Sympy: This is a library that works well if you want to do some things in symbolic mathematics.

6. Pandas: This is the number one part that you need to use because it is going to include all of the analysis and the data structure needed to make machine learning successful.

The different extensions and modules that you can use with SciPy are known collectively as SciKits. This is why the module that provides us with the learning algorithms needed are going to be called the Scikit-Learn library.

The vision that is going to come in with this library will include a lot of support and robustness than you can find with some of the other topics that you explore. This is a good thing because both of these are going to require some higher levels to make sure that the production system works the way we expect and want. When going through this process, there has to be a deeper focus on the concerns, including ease of use, the collaboration, documentation, code quality, and performance, or it isn't going to work the way we want.

Knowing Some of the Features of This Library

At this point, we have talked a bit about this library, but we haven't gone into any of the details of the features, or the reasons that you would choose to work with this system over one of the others. When you decide to work with this particular library, you are probably going to be curious as to what it is all about, and even why some people want to work with this while learning and working with machine learning.

The Scikit-Learn library is going to be the most focused on modeling data. It isn't going to take that much time to look at how to summarize the data, load the data, or manipulate the data. If you want to work through these three topics, then you would want to spend some time in the libraries of NumPy and Pandas. However, some of the features you can get through this library, and some of the different models that are available here include:

1. Supervised models: This Scikit-Learn library is going to provide you with many linear models (mostly generalized) that can work well in machine learning. This could include some of the algorithms like a discriminate analysis, decision trees, lazy methods, the Naïve Bayes, support vector machines, and neural networks, to name a few.

2. Manifold learning: These are important because they are often going to be used to help depict and summarize some of the multi-dimensional data that may seem hard to get through for a beginner.

3. Parameter tuning: This is a tool that you may find useful when you want to learn more and get more out of your supervised models.

4. Feature selection: This is going to be a part of the library that is going to help you see, and then identify meaningful attributes from creating a new supervised model.

5. Feature extraction: This one is helpful because it is going to help you learn how to define the attributes in text data and images presented to the machine.

6. Ensemble methods: You will enjoy this feature because it is going to be helpful when you combine the predictions that you have from several models of supervised learning, and then have these all come together to form a new prediction using all that information.

7. A reduction in dimensionality: This is a method found in this library that is helpful when you would like to find a way to reduce the number of attributes needed in data to help with feature selection, visualization, and summarization. A good example of how this works is going to be the principal component analysis.

8. Data sets: This is helpful because it is the place where you can test some of the sets of data that you have, the ones that are going to generate the right sets of data with the right properties so you can do a bit of investigating.

9. Cross-validation: There are times when you will want to figure out whether a model is giving you accurate results or not. The

cross-validation will help you get an estimation on how well that model is going to perform on the data that you have without it even seeing that data.

10. Clustering This is where you can group any data that doesn't have a label, such as with the K-means method that we will discuss a bit later.

These are just a few of the benefits that you are going to be able to get when it comes to working with this library. It is a strong library to use, one that is going to provide you with the results and answers that you want to many supervised machine learning algorithms. Without this in place, it is going to be hard to figure out how you would like to do these algorithms at all and determine if the information you get is accurate when you work with machine learning.

Chapter 6: Working with the K-Nearest Neighbors Algorithm

There are a lot of different types of algorithms that you can work with when it comes to the idea of machine learning. Some of these are going to be easy to work with, and some a bit more complicated—but they can handle information that is a bit more complex as well. The first algorithm that we are going to explore here is known as the K-Nearest Neighbors or the KNN algorithm.

The KNN algorithm is going to be a supervised machine learning—hence, we will take some time to understand what this is all about a bit more. When you work with this algorithm a bit more, you are going to notice that you will use it when you want to search through any data that you already have to find the k most similar examples of any instance that you would like to work with. Once you can do this well, then the algorithm can move into the data set and will look through and summarize the information that you have. When this algorithm is done, it is going to provide you with the results so that you can make the right predictions for your needs.

Any time a programmer decides to work with this model, they are going to find that the learning they see is more competitive overall. The reason why this happens and works is that there

243

will be competition between the parts or elements. These compete against each other to ensure that, based on any of the data you present to it, you will get the best predictions.

As we go through this guidebook and explore a bit more about the different algorithms, you may start to notice how the KNN algorithm is different than some of the other options. For example, many experts like to avoid this approach because they think it is a lazier option, mainly because it isn't going to create any of the models that you may need for the information—unless you specifically go through and ask it for some new predictions. Depending on what data you are working with, this may be a good thing because it ensures that when predictions are made, it is using the most up to date and accurate information.

If your program had just gotten into the habit of trying to make predictions automatically on regular intervals, or when you added in new data, that could be helpful in some situations. But if you would instead look at the data when it is the most convenient to yourself, or you want to divide up the data into certain customer groups, then the KNN algorithm and the methods attached to it are going to be the best.

The KNN algorithm can be a good one to work with because it provides you with a lot of benefits. When you are working with this algorithm, you can go through the data and work on cutting out some of the noise. In some cases, the more data that you have, the more noise that you have to get through. And this algorithm is particularly good when you have a large amount of data to go through. It can sort through as much data as you would like, and give you some accurate predictions, which is a lot more than what some of the other algorithms are capable of.

Now, as you are working on this, you may notice that one of the biggest issues that can come up when you work on this algorithm is that the costs of computing the information are going to be a bit higher than what you see with other algorithms. This is going to occur because this algorithm takes the time to look through each data point that you have, rather than taking those data points and clustering them together. This can sometimes give you the best predictions, but the costs are sometimes too high to make it worth it.

When Do I Want to Use the KNN Algorithm?

The KNN algorithm is a nice one to work with because it works well with both the classification and the regression problems you have when it comes to prediction. This makes it a very useful tool to go with. With that said, it is going to be used mostly with classification problems. When you are evaluating this technique and trying to figure out if it is the right one for you or not, there are going to be three things to consider, and these will include:

1. The power of prediction of this algorithm

2. The time it takes to do the calculations

3. How easy it will be to interpret the output that you have

When you take a look at this algorithm and compare it to other options, including algorithms for logistic regression, random forests, and CART, you will find that it is going to fair well with all of these parameters. Often, you will find out that this algorithm is used because it is easy to interpret the provided results, and the calculation costs are going to be lower?

How Do I Use the Algorithm?

Since we have been talking about this algorithm for a bit now, you are probably curious as to how you would work with and use this algorithm to see the results with your data. There are a few steps that you will want to consider when it comes to this algorithm and making sure that it works the way that you want, including:

1. Load the data into the algorithm so that you can read through.

2. Initialize the value that you are going to use and rely on `for k`.

3. When you are ready to get the predicted class, iteration from one to the total number of the data points that you use for training, you can use the following steps to help.

a. Start by calculating the distance that is in between each of your test data, and each row of your training data. We are going to work with the Euclidean distance as our metric for distance since it's the most popular method. Some of the other metrics that you may choose to work with here include the cosine and Chebyshev.

b. Sort the calculated distances going in ascending order, based on their distance values.

c. Get the k rows from the sorted array.

d. Get the most frequent class for these rows.

e. Return the class prediction.

Why Would We Consider This Algorithm Non-Parametric?

This is a question that a lot of beginners are going to have when they get started with this algorithm. When we look at what it means for an algorithm to be non-parametric, it means that we are not making any assumptions of the way that the distribution of the data is done. These methods won't have a fixed number of parameters that must be met in the model.

With this in mind, when we have the KNN algorithm, the model parameters are going to grow with the training data set. An excellent way to think about this whole process is that each training case is going to be more of a parameter of the model, and that is basically how this algorithm is going to work.

Is There a Difference Between the KNN and the K-Mean Algorithm?

When we get to the next chapter, you will discuss an algorithm known as the K-means algorithm, and this can be confusing for those who are just getting into the ideas of machine learning. There are a few differences that do come up with these two methods, and they will include:

1. K-means is more of a technique that you can use when you want to do some unsupervised learning projects. It isn't going to have any variables present that are dependent. But with KNN, you will have some variables that are dependent present.

2. K-means is going to use clustering to split up the data points and then look at these clusters rather than each data point.

When Are Some Times That KNN Will Be Useful?

Several different algorithms work well with the model of KNN. So, why would you want to choose to use some of the algorithms over some of the others, when you have so many options to choose from. There are always some benefits and negatives that come with each algorithm that you choose to go with, but some of the benefits that you will enjoy with the KNN algorithm will include:

1. It can work well with problems, even if they are considered multi-class.

2. You can apply this algorithm to both regressive problems and those that are classification.

3. There aren't any assumptions that come up with the data. This ensures that you get the information that you want, rather than having any assumptions in the place causing some issues.

4. It is an easy algorithm to work with. It is easy to understand, especially if you are new to the machine learning process.

However, there are more options of algorithms that you can work with because the KNN algorithm isn't going to be perfect in every situation that you go to. Some of the negatives that come with using the KNN algorithm includes:

1. It is going to be computationally and memory intensive; expensive. If you don't have the right system and the right amount of space to work with them, it is going to make it more difficult to see the results that you want from this algorithm.

2. If there are a lot of independent variables that you are going to work with, you will find that the KNN algorithm is going to struggle.

3. The KNN algorithm isn't going to work that well if you have any rare event, or skewed, target variables.

4. Sensitive to the scale of data.

Now, if you are working on a problem, you are going to have a small value of k that will then lead you to deal with a bigger variance in the predictions that come up. Also, when you set a more significant value to the k, there are sometimes going to be problems with a large model bias that you need to be aware of from the beginning.

One thing to be aware of here is that there are going to be times when the computer programmer has to go through and create some dummy variables so they can figure out the categorical variables here. This is going to be something that you do instead of the original categorical variables. This is different than working with regression because you could work with the k dummies, instead of having to work with the (k-1).

For example, you may go through this and create a new categorical variable that is known as the Department. Then, inside of this category, you have five new levels that are unique to that one. Because of this, each of the dummies variables are going to have one against its department and else 0.

What Are the Steps to Find the K Value?

And the final thing that we need to focus on in this guidebook can find the optimal or best value of K. The best way to do this is through some cross-validation. It is going to be so important to take the time to complete cross-validation to estimate the error that may be present in the algorithm. This is a simple thing to do because you need to hold out a subset of your set of training from the process of building a model.

Cross-validation, which is also called 10-fold validation, means that the computer programmer has to go through and randomly divide up the training set so that you have ten groups, or folds, while also trying to get these groups to end up fairly close in size. From that, you can use up to 90 percent of your data to train your choice of model. The final 10 percent is going to be saved behind so that you can validate the model at hand.

You will also have what is known as a misclassification rate. You will need to pay attention to this and compute it using validation data of ten percent saved earlier. This procedure is going to go through and repeat itself ten times. Each of these observations is done to validate the information that you want. You will end up with ten different estimates, along with their validation error, and these are averaged out to give you the K value that you need.

Chapter 7: Understanding K-Means Clustering

The next thing that we need to explore here is the algorithm for k-means clustering. This is a great algorithm to use with machine learning, and it can help out a lot with the kind of programming that you do. The basic idea that comes with this is that you can take the data from your system—the type that hasn't been labeled yet—and then put it together into clusters.

Clustering is going to be n unsupervised machine learning. It is going to be applied when your data doesn't come with labels—and the goal of using this algorithm rather than one of the others available is to make it easier to find the various groups or related clusters that are already present in the data.

The main goal of a programmer working with these clusters is that the objects that end up together in one cluster should be closely related to one another, and they are not going to have a lot of similarities to those that are in other clusters. The similarity here is going to be some metric that will show how strong this relationship is between the data objects.

The field of data mining is going to use this clustering quite a bit. This is, especially true if you are doing explorations. But this is not the only field that is going to benefit from this algorithm. You could also use it in fields like data compression, information retrieval, image analysis, pattern recognition, and bioinformatics.

The algorithm can work to form some clusters of data based on how similar the different values of data are. You will then go through and specify what you would like the value of K to be, which will be the number of clusters that you would like the algorithm to make from your data. This algorithm can start by selecting a centroid value that goes with each of the clusters, and then it will go through a total of three steps, including:

1. You will want to start with the Euclidian distance between each data instance and the centroids for all of the clusters.

2. Assign the instances of data to the cluster of centroid with the nearest distance possible.

3. Calculate the new centroid values, depending on the mean values of the coordinates of the data instances from the corresponding cluster.

Working with the K-Means Clustering Algorithm

To work with this algorithm, the input to use for the k-means is going to be found on the matrix X. You can then go through and add in some organization of your choice to ensure that the rows you create are a different sample, while each of the columns are going to include a different factor or feature that you would like to consider. To ensure this is going to happen, you have to focus on two main steps.

For the first part, you need to take some time to choose the centers that will make up the individual clusters. If you are looking through the data and you are not sure about where you should put these centers, you may have to start with some random points for this to see what happens. If you do this and things don't seem to be matching up that well, you can go back through and change it up and see if a new center point is going to work better.

The second step that we need to focus on is going to be the main loop. After you have the chosen centers in place, you can then decide which cluster all of the points of data need to go to. You can look at all of the samples that you have to help you figure out which of the clusters the point of data is going to belong to.

From this point, you will need to go through and do some recalculations on the centers of your clusters. You will need to do this based on the points that you assigned for each part. To make this happen, you will need to grab all of your samples and then figure out what the mean is for these samples. And once you can come up with this answer, then you have the k-means.

You will need to go through these steps until you can make convergence happen with this algorithm. There are not going to be more changes to the cluster centers once this happens. For the most part, depending on how much data you are starting with, this is going to be done in five steps or less. But if you have a lot of data points that have a significant variance, then it is possible that you will need to do it in more steps.

To understand what is going on, let's take a look at how the k-means is going to work.

```
- - -    - ^ -

| 1 |    | 2 |

- - -    - - -

|    |    |
```

```
|    |

|    |

_  *  _    _  _  _

|  3  |    |  4  |


_  _  _    _  _  _
```

This is going to be our initialization point. Here, we will have four vectors that are going to be labeled as 1, 2, 3, and 4. The two cluster centers, which are k=2, have been randomly assigned in this one to points 2 and 3. We used the (*) and the (^) signs to help denote these. It is now time to start with the main loop.

The first step we need to complete during this point is to decide which cluster of our points is going to head over to. Looking above, we will be able to see that both point one and point three are going to be the centers of the clusters on the left because they are both going to be closer to that one than the center cluster. And then, the center points on the right are going to be both points 2 and 4.

The second thing we need to work with here is to do our recalculation. This needs to be done with the centers of the clusters and will be based on the points that are inside each cluster. The (*) cluster is going to be the one that moves between points 1 and points 2 because this ends up being the main points. The same thing will happen with the (^) cluster, but it will move between points two and four. It is pretty easy to come up with the mean for these two points because of the lower amount of data points, but with more complex data, you would be able to use an algorithm to make it happen. For this example, you would need to use the following code:

```
 _ _ _    _ ^ _

| 1 |    | 2 |

 _ _ _    _ _ _

|   |

*     ^

|   |

 _ * _   _ _ _

| 3 |   | 4 |

 _ _ _   _ _ _
```

You will not see any changes happen in the subsequent iterations, so for this example, we are going to be all done.

The Difference Between Fuzzy and Soft K-Means

As you are working on these, you may notice that when you are working with the k-means, they are going to be sensitive as you move them, especially to what is known as the initialization. But how do we fix this so that the areas aren't so sensitive, and you will be able to get some accurate answers that you are able to work on?

There are several strategies that you can use with this one, but one of the best is to go through and restart the k-means at least two times. When you do this, you can compare the results and see which one provides you with the best results when it is all done with. We will take a look at how to do this in the next section. But it allows us to know the cost function and how it is going to be affected, and we can then compare the results and figure out which result is the best one to use.

As you do this, you may find that one of the methods that are going to make it easier to get through any challenges, and will ensure that you find the best results to add in information that is known as a membership that is fuzzy to each class, and see what is going on in that matter.

For example, your fuzzy point may end up being able to fit in 60 percent of your first cluster, along with matching up to 40 percent of the information in the second cluster. You would then use the process of the soft k-means to make adjustments to the algorithm you used before. The first part of it is going to be the same, but you need to make sure that the first k-cluster centers go back to the random points that are a part of your data. But the changes that you will see can come inside some of the loops that you write.

To make this happen, we need to go through and write out some of the responsibilities of the clusters. The best formula to use to make this happen and work out includes:

```
r(kn) = exp[ -b * d(m(k), x(n)) ] / sum[j=1..K] { exp[
-b * d(m(j), x(n)) ] }
```

From here, you can see that the `r(k,n)` is going to work out as a fraction, some number that is in between 0 and 1, where you can interpret the hard k-means or the regular k-means to be the case where `r(k,n)` is always exactly equal to 0 or 1. The `d(*,*)` can be any valid distance metric, but the Euclidean or squared Euclidean distances are the ones that are used the most.

Then for the second step, we are going to work on a formula that is similar to the hard k-means, but we are recalculating the means based on the responsibilities that we want to send with it. The algorithm that we are going to use for this includes:

```
m(k)  =  sum[n=1..N]  {  r(k,n)* x(n)  ]  /  sum[n-1..N]  {
r(k,n) }
```

So, when you consider the algorithm above, you will see that it is similar to the weighted mean. This is going to show you that if the $r(k,n)$ is higher, then the mean is going to be more important to the cluster of k. When you see this, it is going to show that this is going to have the biggest influence on the calculation of the mean. But if the mean is higher when you look at the algorithm, you will know that the opposite is true.

What Is the K-Means Objective Function?

Just like what we have discussed about supervised learning, you must make sure that you spend some of your time looking at and talking about the objective function that you wish to get the most out of with your unsupervised learning. To get started with this idea, we will need to use what is known as the

Euclidean distance to make it easier to measure the distance of each center. The function that we will need to use to figure this out includes:

```
J  =  sum[n=1..N]  {sum[k=1..K]  {  r(k,n)  ||  m(k)  =  x(n)
||^2} }
```

What all of this means is that you are working with the squared distance that was weighted through the responsibilities that it is given. Hence, if the $x(n)$ part ends up being far away from the mean of your k cluster, hopefully, the responsibility that goes with this one is set to be quite low. What happens then is known as a coordinate descent. What this is going to mean is that we are looking to move in the direction of a smaller J concerning just one of the variables at a time. We know that this is something that happened here because we went through and updated one single variable at a time.

Now, when you take a look back at all of this, you will see that there is a bit of a mathematical guarantee that all of the iterations can result in the objective function that you work with going down. If you continue to do this for long enough, and you are properly doing the algorithm, you will find that the points are going to converge together.

Keep in mind that just because you can see a convergence show up doesn't mean that they are going to necessarily come up with the global minimum that you are looking for. The numbers will go off the patterns that show up there, and they will spend time focusing on math, and less about what you may think is the most important. Going through and reading through the results and making sure that they work how you want, and retrying the whole process a few times to see if it comes up with different results can help to fix any issues this can bring up.

How to Add in the K-Means?

In this chapter, we have closely look at k-means, and how this algorithm can work, along with the different ways that this algorithm is used to create the right solution to your program. Now that this is done, it is time to implement in some of the ideas that we have talked about, with the help of machine learning skills and Python to ensure that this can work. And the best way to make all of this come together is to implement the soft k-means into your code.

But, how are we supposed to make sure that this happens? For this to work, you have to make sure that you have your standard imports in place, and the functions of the utilities ready. This will be pretty much the same thing as the

Euclidean distance as well as the function of cost put together. The formula that can help you figure out this information is going to be below:

```
import numpy as np

import matplotlib.pyplot as plt


def d(u, v):

diff = u - v

return diff.dot(diff)



def cost(X, R, M):

cost = 0

for k in xrange(len(M)):

for n in xrange(len(X)):

cost += R[n,k]*d(M[k], X[n])

return cost
```

Once you have taken the time to add this part into the compiler and you use it to define your function so that it can run the k-means algorithm before it plots out the results. This will mean that you will end up with a scatterplot of the information. And the colors that are there will represent the amount of membership of the information found in each cluster. To make this happen, you need to work with the code below:

```
def plot_k_means(X, K, max_iter=20, beta=1.0):

N, D = X.shape

M = np.zeros((K, D))

R = np.ones((N, K)) / K



# initialize M to random

for k in xrange(K):

M[k] = X[np.random.choice(N)]



grid_width = 5

grid_height = max_iter / grid_width

random_colors = np.random.random((K, 3))
```

```
plt.figure()


costs = np.zeros(max_iter)

for i in xrange(max_iter):

# moved the plot inside the for loop

colors = R.dot(random_colors)

plt.subplot(grid_width, grid_height, i+1)

plt.scatter(X[:,0], X[:,1], c=colors)


# step 1: determine assignments / resposibilities

# is this inefficient?

for k in xrange(K):

for n in xrange(N):

R[n,k] = np.exp(-beta*d(M[k], X[n])) / np.sum( np.exp(-
beta*d(M[j], X[n])) for j in xrange(K) )


# step 2: recalculate means

for k in xrange(K):

M[k] = R[:,k].dot(X) / R[:,k].sum()
```

```
costs[i] = cost(X, R, M)

if i > 0:

if np.abs(costs[i] - costs[i-1]) < 10e-5:

break



plt.show()
```

Notice in this one that both the R and the M are going to have their matrices. The R is going to be a new matrix because it can hold onto two different indices—n and k. But the M will also become a matrix because it is going to include the D-dimensional vectors of K. The beta variable is going to be there because it is responsible for controlling how spread-out or fuzzy the memberships of the cluster are, and it is known as the hyperparameter. From this, we can create a new main function that will create the random clusters, and then calls up the functions that we defined above. The code that you will need to use to make all of this work well together includes:

```
def main():

# assume 3 means

D = 2 # so we can visualize it more easily
```

```
s = 4 # separation so we can control how far apart the
means are

mu1 = np.array([0, 0])

mu2 = np.array([s, s])

mu3 = np.array([0, s])


N = 900 # number of samples

X = np.zeros((N, D))

X[:300, :] = np.random.randn(300, D) + mu1

X[300:600, :] = np.random.randn(300, D) + mu2

X[600:, :] = np.random.randn(300, D) + mu3


# what does it look like without clustering?

plt.scatter(X[:,0], X[:,1])

plt.show()


K = 3 # luckily, we already know this

plot_k_means(X, K)
```

```
# K = 5 # what happens if we choose a "bad" K?

# plot_k_means(X, K, max_iter=30)



# K = 5 # what happens if we change beta?

# plot_k_means(X, K, max_iter=30, beta=0.3)




if __name__ == '__main__':

main()
```

With the formulas above, you will be able to work with the k-means algorithm, and you should have a better understanding of how this works. Open up your compiler and work on some of these codes and getting a bit of practice with writing your codes in Python. You will find that this can sharpen your skills and makes it so much easier for you to get the expected results from your machine learning.

Chapter 8 What Are Support Vector Machines?

Now that we have considered other methods that work well with machine learning, it is time to learn more about support vector machine or SVM. This is going to be something that you can often utilize for many of the machine learning challenges that come up—both with classification and regression issues. When you work with this one, a lot of works done on problems that are more classified can be a bit tricky. However, the algorithm for SVM will help out with this.

When you want to do some work with the SVM algorithm, you need to take each of your items in the data set and plat them so that they come to just one point on your n-dimensional space. The N is going to be the number of features that you would like to use with this one. Then you can take the value of these various features and make it so that it translates over to the values that tend to show up on your coordinates. The next step, once this point has been reached, is to determine where the hyperplane is going to be. This part is crucial because it will show you what differences are there in your classes.

When you are working with this algorithm, you may notice that it is possible for more than one of these support vectors to show up. You will not be able to use all of these, or your information will end up being confused. You want to work with just the SVM so that you can separate this information into classes, and then you will know which one to focus on in the line and hyperplane.

Here, you have reached a point where a lot of the information may not make all that much sense. And you may not even know why you would like to learn and use SVM in the first place. But it is a powerful algorithm that you can work with, and there are a few steps that a beginner can work with to make sure that they are getting the full benefits of all this.

So, to help us start here, we need to look at our hyperplane. As you go through all of this, you may notice that there are a few different hyperplanes that you can pick out from. And there is also another challenge that is added here in that you want to make sure that you understand all of the options, ensuring that you choose the best one for your needs. But even though you are going to end up with a few different options, there are some simple steps that you can utilize to help you pick the right one for your needs. The steps to follow to make this happen includes

- We are going to start with three hyperplanes that we will call 1, 2, and 3. Then we spend time figuring out which hyperplane is right so that we can classify the star and the circle.

- The good news is there is a pretty simple rule that you can follow so that it becomes easier to identify which hyperplane is the right one. The hyperplane that you want to go with will be the one that segregates your classes the best.

- That one was easy to work with, but in the next one, our hyperplanes of 1, 2, and 3 are all going through the classes, and they segregate them in a similar manner. For example, all of the lines or these hyperplanes are going to run parallel with each other. From here, you may find that it is hard to pick which hyperplane is the right one.

- For the above issue, we will need to use what is known as the margin. This is the distance that occurs between the hyperplane and the nearest data point from either of the two classes. Then you will be able to get some numbers that can help you out. These numbers may be closer together, but they will point out which hyperplane is going to be the best.

As you can see, we just did an example above, and it is a great one to show you how to work with the SVM algorithm and get the most out of your machine learning project. When you would like to take a look at the different points of data that you have available, and you notice that there is a good margin that can point out separation, then this algorithm is the best one for you. Also, you will find that this model is effective and helps you increase any of the time that you are working on this project.

As a programmer, likely, you are not going to use this model all of the time. But even with this fact, working with this technique can help you to do a lot with machine learning. It helps you to use a subset of your points for training so that you can figure out where the connections are and how to make them work.

While several benefits come with using this method, depending on what data points and what project you are working with, there will still be some times when SVM may not work for you. If you are using a really large set of data, this model runs into issues being as accurate as you would like. The training time that comes with these bigger data sets is high, and you may not be able to get the information that you want as quickly as you would like.

Chapter 9: Using Neural Networks

The next topic that we are going to take a look at with machine learning is going to be the neural networks. These are going to also fall into the category of unsupervised machine learning. These networks are used often because they will ensure you can look through your data and notice if there are any patterns present in the information. This is going to be done at different levels, and it is much more effective and faster than what the human eye can do on its own.

When we look at the neural networks, each of the layers that you go through will get the algorithm to stop and see if there is some pattern found in the image that it is looking through. If the network isn't able to find a new pattern once they go down another layer, then it will start taking the necessary steps to help it move on to the next layer. This process continues through one layer after another, until all of the layers are created. The program, if it is doing its job rightly, is going to be able to give you a good prediction back about what is inside the image that you scanned.

There are a few things that could happen when you enter this point, based on how the program is working. If the algorithm was able to go through the process above, and it did a good job at sorting through the layers, it will then provide you with a prediction. If the program is right in its prediction, the neurons of this system just like the neurons in the brain are going to become stronger.

The reason that this works so well is that the program decided to work with artificial intelligence, which allowed it to make strong associations between the object and the patterns that it found. The more times that the system can look at a picture and come back with the right answer, the more efficient it is going to be the next time you use it.

To find out how this works will require us to look a bit closer at how the neural networks work together. For example, let's say that you have set out to create a new program that can hold onto a picture, which will be your input. And then it can look through the various layers of that picture until it figures out that the image inside is a car.

If you have gone through and coded this in the right way, the program can predict that the picture is that of a car. The program will be able to come up and present you with this prediction based on some of the features that it knows, from experience, belongs to a car. It could look at the headlights, the placement of the doors, the license plate, and more to come up with this prediction.

When you are looking at your skills in conventional coding and what is all available to you through this, then this process is going to be a difficult one. You will find that with machine learning, and the neural networks algorithm, you will be able to get this to work without too many problems.

But how do we get this algorithm to work? To make this happen, you need first to make sure the program has an image of a car to compare the newer image to. The neural network will take this learning picture and look it over. It would be able to start with the very first layer. In this case, this is going to be the edges on the outside of the car. From there, the program would go through other layers that are going to help the neural network learn whether any characteristics are unique to the picture and will tell it that a car is in the picture.

If the program has worked with trial and error, and it is good at doing this job, it is going to make the right prediction. And the more pictures of cars that you provide to this program, the better it is going to get at finding the car and predicting it, and the more minute details it will notice.

Depending on the picture you are working with, there could be a lot of potential layers that come with this algorithm. The good news here is that the more details and the more layers that your neural network can find, the better the accuracy it comes with when it predicts the car and the type of car. If the neural network is accurate and does a good job with the predictions, it can learn from these lessons. It is going to remember what it learned as it went through the layers and can store that information to use later on. If it does need to look at another similar picture in the future, it will be able to make a rapid prediction in the process.

Any time that a programmer wants to work with the neural network algorithm, you will often be working with things like face recognition software and other similar projects. When this happens, all of the information that you and the program need won't be available ahead of time. But you can use this method to teach the system the best way to recognize the right faces in the image. You can also use this one to help with different types of animals, to define models of cars, and so much more.

As you can imagine reading through this chapter, there are a lot of different advantages that come with this particular model when working on machine learning. One of the advantages that you are going to notice is that you can utilize these methods without having to control the statistics of the algorithm. Even if you need to use it without the statistics being available, the neural network will still be able to finish the work for you. The reason that this ends up working so well is that both the dependent and the independent variable are going to be nonlinear.

There are a few times when you will not want to work with this method. One of the main reasons that programmers would choose not to go with a neural network is that it is also one of those models that has a high computing cost to get the information. For some of the smaller businesses who are interested in working with machine learning and doing this kind of technology, the cost is going to take too much time, computational power, and money and they will need to look at some other algorithms instead.

Chapter 10: The Random Forest Algorithm

When you start to learn about machine learning, there are going to be many instances where you hear about decision trees and random forests. Both of these are essential algorithms that you should learn how to use, and you will find that they often work together to help you get the right results with your data sets. In this chapter, we are going to begin our exploration with some decision tree information to learn more about them—then, we will move on to the random forests and how they can be compared and work with the decision trees.

First on the list is the decision trees. These are efficient tools for data if you would like to compare and contrast two choices, especially if those two choices are very different. You can then use the information that you were able to gather to pick out the right one to follow, and in the process, grow and improve your business. When you see a presentation of the various options presented to you, you will be able to utilize the algorithm for a decision tree to see the possible outcomes. This is a great way to make predictions and come up with the best decisions for your needs.

The neat thing about decision trees is that there are a few different ways that you can work with them—many of those in machine learning like to work with these decision trees for random or categorical variables. However, there are going to be times when you can use decision trees to help with problems of classification. To make sure you do this process accurately and you have a good decision tree, you will need to take up all of the sets of data that you plan to work with, and split them up into at least two sets. And in each of these sets, the data needs to be similar. Once you are done with that, the sets can be sorted more to help you figure out what is important and what isn't.

So, this can bring up the idea that this is a hard algorithm to work with. To be certain that you are doing the decision trees in the rightly, and that they are going to work for you, you first need to check out this example. For this one, we are going to take a look at a class that has 60 people inside of it. There are three variables, all that are considered independent of each other, that we need to consider about these students. And the independent variables are going to include class, height, and gender. Also, as you look over the information about the students, you see that half of the class doesn't like soccer and doesn't like to spend their time with this sport.

Now that we have a bit of information to go from, it is time to see how the decision tree can help us with this. Given this information about the students who like to play soccer, you decide that it is time to create a new model that will help you figure out which of these students likes soccer, and which ones don't. This is possible with the decision trees.

To help us make this model, the decision tree needs to look at all of the students, and then find an excellent way to divide them up into the groups where they belong. The variables that need to be used here would include the height, gender, and class. The goal here is that when everything is done, you will be able to have a homogenous set of students, ones who like to do the same things together.

When you are working with a decision tree, there are going to be several algorithms that can be used along with this. And each of them will make it possible to split up the data that you have. Working with the right algorithm will help you divide things up into subsets that you can work with, and then they will produce good outcomes that are as homogenous as possible so that you can make the right decisions for your needs. Remember that you can add in more subsets if the situation needs it. For this particular example, though, we are working with two, which includes the students who play soccer and the ones who don't like soccer.

This is a simplified version of this idea, but there are times when you will be able to work with the decision trees to go through some complex data and sort out the points based on their differences and their similarities. These decision trees are going to provide you with the data that you need, and then you can take that data and make some informed and smart decisions for your business.

Yes, in the past, business owners would use the knowledge that they had about the industry and their intuition to help them make decisions about how to act in the future. But decision trees are often going to make the work easier, and are more accurate than what you are going to see with traditional decision-making forms. The decision tree can help you to look through more information, can sort it out easier, and can make it easy to compare the different options rather than trying to do it all on your own.

Starting with the Random Forests

There are also going to be times when a decision tree isn't quite what you need with your project. This is often going to happen, and when it does, you may want to take a bit of time to work with the algorithm that is called a random forest algorithm. These algorithms are going to be popular for you to work with, so if you would like to do machine learning regularly, or you plan to go into the field of data science, then this is a machine learning algorithm that you need to learn more about.

Since these random forest algorithms are so popular, you can guess that the algorithm can be used to help out with a lot of challenges here. For example, if you would like to work with tasks that can look through the data and explore it a bit, like dealing with information when the data is missing, or treating for any information outliers that are present, then the random forest is going to be the number one algorithm to use for this.

There are a few times when you are doing some machine learning process, and then the random forest will need to be brought out. This is because the random forest is going to be perfect when it comes to providing you with some good results—and often, they can complete the job of other algorithms or do the job better. Some of the different benefits and uses of these random forests that will help you see the best results will include:

Any time that a computer programmer is trying to do their own sets for training, they will find that all of the objects that are on the inside of the set can be generated randomly. And there are times when it can be replaced if your random tree thinks that this is something necessary and essential for your needs.

If there are M input variable amounts, then this means that the $m<M$ will be specified right from the beginning. Also, this information is going to be a constant help throughout the project. The reason we need to remember this is because it means that each tree that you have has been picked at random for their variable using the M from before.

The goal of these trees, no matter how many of them you end up with, is to help you find the split that is the best for the "m" variable.

As your tree starts to grow more, all of them are going to get as big as they can with the data you have. Remember that these are not trees that can take the information out, or do any pruning of themselves.

The forest you get from these random trees can be a good resource to use because it can predict specific outcomes for you. It is going to take over this job because it takes all of the predictions that you get from the created trees, and then it can select the average for the regression, or provides you with the consensus that you will get during a classification challenge.

You will find that these random forests are an excellent tool for programmers to use when adding in a bit more data science to their machine learning. And from the information above, there is a lot of advantages to working with these random forests, rather than using the other available algorithms.

The first significant benefit that you will notice with the random forest is that they can deal with all machine learning challenges, whether they are regression or classification challenges. Many times, the other machine learning algorithms that you will work with can be *either* a regression solver or a classification solver—not both of them.

Another great benefit that comes with these random forests is that they can work when you need to sort through a large amount of data. And you get to go through and add in hundreds of thousands of variables (if it is needed), and the algorithm is still able to handle the work. Of course, it isn't that likely that these many variables are needed when doing this, but it is nice to know the amount of power that is used with the random forest algorithm.

Just like with all of the other algorithms that we have talked about so far in this guidebook, there are a few negatives when it comes to doing random forests. First, even though the random forest can do some regression problems in machine learning, they are not going to be helpful when it comes to the predictions that you should put in when it concerns the training data. It also can't talk about the ranges that are present there either.

What this means is that there are times when the random forest can make a few predictions that are helpful to you. And there are some times when you can use these predictions to help you make some fantastic business decisions. But this algorithm is still going to come with a few limitations because you won't be able to go past the ranges that you provide the algorithm, and this decreases the amount of accuracy that you are going to get.

Chapter 11: What Are Recurrent Neural Networks?

We spent some time earlier in this guidebook talking about neural networks, and how they work to go through the different layers of pictures to provide you with the information that you need concerning what is in that picture. Now, we are going to take this a bit further and talk more about an algorithm that is known as recurrent neural networks.

To help us get started with this one, we need to take a closer look at the human brain. When we look at the human brain, it is understood that we aren't going to restart the way we think, going back to nothing each second. You can learn something, and then use that knowledge and build upon it all of the time. Whether that knowledge is from your childhood or five minutes ago, you have to start from nothing each time this happens. You can keep on learning, building upon each experience that occurs in your life to increase your knowledge.

When we look at the traditional neural network with machine learning that we looked at earlier, this process isn't able to do the same thing as the brain. And this can sometimes be a significant shortcoming based on the project that you want to work with. For example, if you would like to do some classification for the event that occurs during a movie, it is hard to do this with the traditional neural network. This is because you wouldn't be able to remember what happened in the move earlier through that algorithm, and you would run into trouble knowing when different things happen.

This can seem like it is going to cause issues with your project severely, but that doesn't have to be the case. The recurrent neural networks that we will explore in this guidebook are meant to be used to address this exact issue that shows up. These are going to be networks that contain loops inside, which allows the information to stick around, rather than leaving. In this method, the loop is there to allow information to pass from one part of the network on over to the next part. A recurrent neural network can be a similar idea as having more than one copy of the same network, and each message is sent over to the right spots.

The nature of this chain is there to reveal that the recurrent neural networks are going to be related very closely with sequences and lists. They are going to be the natural architecture of the neural network to use for this data. And you will find that in your programming, you can work with these quite a bit. For example, over the past few years, programmers found success when they were able to apply these ideas to a variety of problems in machine learning including with speech recognition, translation, captioning, and language modeling.

Now, while some benefits come with this process, it is important to realize that there are going to be some limitations that come with this network. The biggest one is that the API is going to have a lot of constraints put onto it. These API's are only going to accept fixed vector sizes as their input, and then they are only able to produce a fixed-sized vector as the output.

This is a big problem, but it is one of the problems that you are going to need to deal with. You may also find that these models are going to perform this mapping with a fixed number of steps computationally, which equals the number of layers that will show up in this particular model. The main reason that these options are going to add in some excitement and something new to the program is that they will allow the programmer to operate their work over a sequence of vectors. This can usually happen with both the output and with the input.

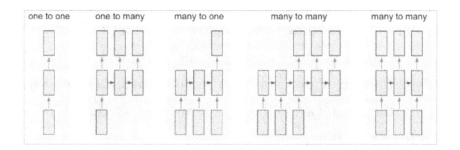

Now, the chart above is going to help us understand more about these recurrent neural networks. Each of the rectangles that you see there will be our vectors, and the arrows are there to show us the functions. When we look at the vectors for input, they are the red ones. And then the vectors for output are going to be blue. Those green vectors are going to be the state of RNN (which we will explore in a minute). So, when we go from the left of this chart over to the right, we can see the following:

1. In the first one, we are looking at what is known as the vanilla mode of processing. This is going to be the processing method that won't use the RNN at all. This is going to include a fixed input and a fixed output. We would also call this one image classification.

2. For the second part, we are looking at the sequence output. This will be what we see with image captioning. This is where you take an image, and then the system can provide you with an output of a sentence describing it.

3. Sequence input is going to be what we see with the third part of the chart. This one is going to be seen as a sentiment analysis that can show us a given sentence and then helps us classify this correctly, either as a positive sentiment or a negative sentiment.

4. The sequence input and output. You will then be able to move on to the fourth box. This is going to help us get closer to what we are looking for here. This is going to be similar to what we see with a machine translation. When the RNN can read out our sentence in English, and then it takes that information and provides you with a sentence, then you reach the fourth part.

5. In the last box, we get to the final part of this process. This is going to be where the input and output of the sequence can be synced together. The classification of the video is going to help us to label the frames that we have—if we decide to go that far.

Notice that when we go through each of these different parts, there are not going to be any constraints put on the length of the sequences that we have to specify ahead of time. This is because this transformation, which is shown with the color of green, is fixed, and we can use it as many times as are needed to finish up this project.

What Is the RNN?

We took a moment to mention the idea of the RNN in the previous section, but now, we need to take some time to explore what all of this is about. In this example here, we are going to work to train the RNN character level language mode. What this ends up meaning is that we will need to provide the

RNN is a large amount of text, and then we will go through with the model of the probability of distribution of the next character that is going to show up in a sequence of previous characters. This ends up being a good thing because it will make sure we can get some text, even if the system is just able to do one character at a time.

As an example, suppose that we had a minimal vocabulary to work with, and just four possible letters (helo). With this information, we want to train the RNN to do a training sequence of "hello" instead. This training sequence is going to be a source of four separate training examples. This may sound a bit complex when we are first getting started, but we will take this step by step to help you see how it works. Some of the things to consider to get this started includes:

1. The probability of getting "e" should be just as likely to occur as getting the letter "h."

2. "l" should be likely in the context of "he."

3. The "l" should also be likely if the system is given the context of "hel."

4. "o" should be likely if the other sequences have happened and the context of "hell" is in place.

Now, we are going to encode each of the characters that occur in the vector working with the "1 of k" in coding (this is going to mean that we will use all zeroes except for a single one at the index of the character in the vocabulary). We will then be able to feed them into the RNN, doing so one at a time, using the function for step to make this happen.

Once all of this has gotten into place, we are going to observe a sequence of 4-dimensional output vectors, with one dimension showing up for each character, which we can then interpret as the confidence that the RNN is able to assign right now to each of the characters that come up in the next sequence at a time. Let's take a look at a diagram that can show up when it is time to run this sequence.

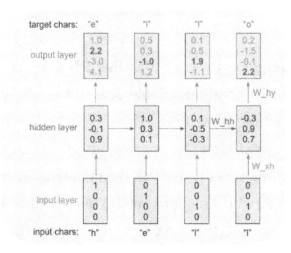

Out of this, we may use an example of seeing that in the first time step, the RNN would see the character of "h", it was able to assign some confidence to this of 1.0, to the next letter turning into "h", 2.2 to getting the letter "e", 3.0 to "l", and 4.1 to "o". Since the training data we are using (which is the string of hello that we talked about above) had the next right character being "e", we want to increase the confidence—or the green color—and then decrease how confident it is in all of the other letters, which are going to be shown in the red above.

The next thing is to go through another step and figure out the character target that we want to have at each of the four steps that we would like this network to assign its confidence to. This can be a bit time consuming to do, but it is going to be helpful because it ensures that we get the right confidence levels to ensure the system will put the correct letters in at the right time.

Since we are going to work with this RNN feature, and it is going to consist of differentiable operations, we will use the back-propagation algorithm. This is going to include an application that is recursive of the chain rules that you should remember from calculus. We will then take this information to figure out the right direction, moving the weights as we need to help us increase the scores on the targets that we want, which are shown in the green and the bold numbers above.

Once we are done doing this work, we will need to go through and do an update of our parameter. This is going to be what we need to help nudge the weights just a bit towards the direction that we would like. If you can take some time to check the inputs that are fed into the RNN end up the same after each update on the parameter, you will find that the scores of the correct characters are going to be higher and that the ones that are not right will go down by a little.

Now, it is possible that you will need to go through and do this process more than ones, and sometimes you will need to do it often, to ensure that it is going to work for you. The number of times that you need to make this happen is going to depend on the complexity of the system. Since the example that we are going to use here is the "hello' code, it won't take that much to get it done.

But since machine learning can be pretty complicated and will need a lot of programming, it is possible that this is going to be complicated enough that you have to go through and do it many times. You have to be prepared to repeat this process until you can get the network to converge correctly, and you can get the predictions to be consistent with the data for training that you are using.

Another option to work with here is a technical explanation. You can do this once you have the classifier that is considered standard for Softmax. This can sometimes be referred to as the cross-entropy loss, on every output vector at the same time. If you can do this, you are training the RNN with a mini-hatch stochastic Gradient Descent, and you may find that you need to add in RMSProp or Adam to make the updates that you do as stable as they can be here.

If you can do these, you will start to notice that the first time that you add in your character as an input of "l," the target is going to be "l." But if you go through and do this again, it is going to be "O." The RNN is going to need to have some help because the input is not going to be enough all on its own. This means that it needs to have a connection that is recurrent to help keep track of the context that will make this task as achievable as possible.

After you do the iterations a few times, you will get to testing—it is time to go through and add in the right characters to the RNN algorithm. As you are training, you should be able to see the distribution and how it will look if you make a specific prediction. The computer programmer needs to take a sample from the given distribution and feed it right back into the algorithm to tell you which letter is going to show up next.

Continue to go through with this process again and again until you can get the right letter that you want, in the correct order.

As you can see, there are going to be many different things that are possible when you decide to work with the algorithm RNN, and many of these are impossible to do if you are working with some of the other algorithms available through machine learning. Using the RNN algorithm is going to open up a lot of doors and will help you to handle more machine learning situations in the process as well.

Chapter 12: Linear Classifiers

As you go through and work with some machine learning, especially when it comes to supervised learning, you may find that two of the most common tasks that are going to be required here will include both the linear regression and the linear classifier. The linear regression is helpful in some situations because it can predict the value of your data—then, the linear classifier is useful because it focuses on the class. While both of these are useful in machine learning, we are going to look at the linear classifier and some of the steps that you will use when you bring this up in machine learning.

You will find out quickly that when you are working on machine learning, these classification problems are very prevalent, and they will take up a minimum of 80 percent of the tasks that you will do in machine learning. Classification aims to predict how probable it is that each class is going to happen given the inputs that you decide to put in, the label (the label is going to be the dependent variables here), and the class.

If your dependent variable or the label only comes in with two classes to work within the beginning, then you know that the algorithm that you are working with is a binary classifier. If you would like to work with a classifier that has more than one class, this means that it will be able to tackle any of the labels with three or more classes.

Let's look at an example of this one. Many of the classification problems that are also considered binary can predict how likely it is that your customer will come back, after making one purchase, and purchase again. But if you would like the system to predict the animal that you have placed into an image, you will instead work with a classification problem that is known as multiclass. This is because there will be more than two types of animals that can show up in the picture.

Measuring Your Linear Classifier Performance

Now, we need to take a look at the linear classifier a bit more and how you can measure how well it can perform. Accuracy is essential with any of the learning algorithms that you work with, and it is one of the best places to start. The performance overall of this classifier is going to be measured using the metric of accuracy—this is how important it is for you.

When we talk about accuracy, it is the measurement of whether the algorithm can collect the proper values that you have, and then it can divide that number by the total number of observations that are present. Looking at an example of this, if you have an accuracy value that is set at 85 percent, this means that your algorithm is going to be right 85 percent of the time, but then it is going to be wrong the other 15 percent. Of course, if you are working with numbers and data, you want to make sure that the accuracy is as high as possible.

As you take a look at the accuracy, you should also note that there is a shortcoming with this metric, and this is never more apparent than when you are looking at a class of imbalance. A set of data that ends up not being balanced is going to occur when the number of observations that show up isn't equal in all of the groups that you have.

To understand this, let's say that you are doing a classification challenge of a rare event with the function of logistics. You would need to think about the classifier that you would like to use, and that will include estimating how many patients died when they were in contact with a disease. In the data, you see that five percent of the infected patients were going to die.

From this information, you would be able to train your chosen classifier to make sure that it can predict the number of deaths is going to occur for those with the disease. Then you can go through and use the metric of accuracy to evaluate how that clinic or hospital is performing. With this example, the classifier can go and look at the information. Maybe it predicts that there are going to be no deaths for the set of data as a whole. This is going to be accurate about 95 percent of the time, which gives it some margin of error.

The next thing that we need to focus on here is something known as the confusion matrix. This is going to be a better way to take a look at how well the classifier can perform compared to the accuracy that you were able to do above. When you decide to bring in the confusion matrix, you will be able to get a visual about how accurate the classifier is by comparing the actual and the predicted classes. The binary confusion matrix is going to consist of squares. If you decide to work with this kind of confusion matrix, there are a few different parts that come   with   it   including

1. TP: This is going to be known as the true positive. This is going to contain all of the predicted values that were predicted correctly as an actual positive.

2. FP: This is going to be the false ones—or the ones that were predicted incorrectly. They were predicted usually as positive, but they were negative. This means that the negative values show up, but they had been predicted ahead of time as positive.

3. FN: This is a false negative. This is when your positive values are predicted as negative.

4. TN: this is going to be the true negative. These are the values that were predicted correctly and predicted as actual negative.

When a computer programmer takes a look at this confusion matrix to use it, they are going to get a lot of information to use. The confusion matrix can help you get a nice clear look at the predicted class, and the actual class, so that you can compare and contrast what is going on with the data that you have.

Are Sensitivity and Precision Important?

The confusion matrix is one of the best things that you can work with when it comes to looking through the linear classification and understanding the information that is in your data. But when you do this kind of matrix, you will find that a lot of information will come your way. These matrices are also going to give you some insights when it comes to a true positive and a false positive in the information that you have. However, even though this is a great thing to work with, there are still some cases when it would be better to go with a more concise metric to help you understand the information at hand.

The first thing that we need to look at here with the metric that you use is precision. The precision metric is important because it shows us how accurate the positive class is going to be. This may sound confusing, but it means that this precision metric is going to provide you a measure of how likely the positive class prediction is going to be correct in the long run. To do this, you can use the formula below to make this easier:

```
Precision = TP / (TP + FP)
```

The maximum amount, or score, that you are going to end up with here is one. And this is going to show up the classifier and be correct when you have a positive value. While precision, and knowing how precise the metric is ahead of time can be super critical to the success that you get, it is not going to be all that you need to look for, mainly because it can ignore the negative class. This metric is something that you would be able to use, but it is more helpful if you pair it up with what is known as the recall metric. The recall is also going to be known as the true positive rate, or the sensitivity rate.

From this point, we also need to have a good idea of the sensitivity that comes with this learning algorithm. This sensitivity can be important because it will let you know the ratio of positive classes that your algorithm can figure out correctly. The metric is a good way to model and take a look at a positive formula that will help you work with this algorithm and figure out its sensitivity will include the following:

```
Recall = TP / (TP + FN)
```

Using TensorFlow and Linear Classifiers Together

Earlier in this guidebook, we took a look at what the TensorFlow library is all about and why it would be a useful option to work with. Now, we are going to take a look at this idea and discuss some of the ways that you can use this library, especially when it comes to a linear classifier algorithm. The first thing that we are going to be able to do to help combine the two of these is to use a data set that is a census.

The whole aim of doing this is to help us use the variable in a census data set to help us come up with a prediction of the income of those people who are going to participate in this data. Note that the income for this example is going to be known as a binary variable.

For this example, we are going to set the variable that is binary at one of the income of the individual, and it is set to be above $50,000. However, if the income ends up being under this dollar amount, then we will need to write out the variable that is binary as 0. The data set that we can work with to make this all happen can be written out in eight variables that are categorical and include the following:

- Native country

- Sex

- Race

- Relationship

- Occupation

- Marital status

- Education

- Place of work

And on top of this, we are going to take a look in this at six of the continuous variables. These are going to include:

- Hours_week

- Capital_loss

- Capital_gain

- Education_num

- Fnlwgt

- Age

Once we have this information, you can open up the TensorFlow library to figure out what the probability is. This probability is going to help us figure out which customers can fit into each group (which ones make more than $50,000 and which ones earn less than $50,000).

In this example, you are going to separate each of your customers into two groups. The first group will be the individuals who listed themselves as making more than $50,000. And the second group is going to be individuals who will make under $50,000. When the individuals are separated into these two groups, you will then be able to look more at their background information, and figure out some information about them like their race, sex, where they work, where they live, and anything else that you would like about them. This can provide some valuable insights for a business to learn more about their customers and how they may purchase things in the future.

Many businesses like to do this because it allows them to learn more about their customers, and ensures that they can figure out who to advertise too. It can also be useful when it comes to customers who come back and make purchases more than once. The business would be able to use this information to figure out how likely it is that a first-time customer is going to come back, and can change up their marketing and advertising to reach these kinds of people more often.

Discriminative Models and Generative Models

At some point, you will need to create some parameters that go with your linear classifier. And when it is time to work with these parameters, two classes or methods can help you with this. These are pretty broad, and they are known as either the generative model or the discriminative model.

Methods that come with the generative model are going to be functions that look at the conditional density. The examples of these types of algorithms that you may use with machine learning will include the Linear Discriminant Analysis, which will assume the Gaussian conditional density models, or you can work with the classifier that relies on the Naïve Bayes algorithm.

The other method that we brought up above is going to be the discriminative model. These are going to be vital because they are going to work to make sure that any output that you get from the program is as high in quality as it can be, especially when you work with the training set. It is possible that when you are doing with the training that you will need to add in some additional terms, but they can cost more and may be able to perform the regularization of the final model that you get. There are a few options that the computer programmer can choose from when they work with discriminative training, and these options will include:

1. Logistic regression: This one is important because it can show us the likelihood estimation of linear classifiers. It is going to do this with the assumption that the observed training set is going to be generated through a binomial model and it is going to depend on the kind of output that the classifier provides to us.

2. Perception: This is a type of algorithm that you would like to use in some of your machine learning because you will use it to fix up any errors that may occur in your training set, which makes it more accurate overall.

3. Support vector machine Remember this one from before? It can work with your discrimination model as well. This is going to be the type of algorithm that you will be able to use and maximize quite a bit. You can use examples that can hose up in

the hyperplane of the decision and in the training set to help with accuracy.

Despite the name that comes with it, the LDA is not going to be one of the options that come with the discriminative models, at least in this method. However, the name is going to make sense if you can compare it to the other algorithms that fit into this model. You will find that this LDA algorithm can fit more in with the supervised machine learning method, and it will instead be there to work on the labels of your data. But then the PCA will be more of an unsupervised machine learning algorithm, and it will go through and, on purpose, ignore all of the labels that you have present there.

In many cases, you will be able to work with discriminative training, but as you do, you will be able to get an accuracy that is much higher compared to the conditional density functions. But, if you do work with those later models, handling the data that is missing in that set is going to be easier. So, as you can see, you have to give and take a bit here. You have to pick whether you want a better accuracy in your information, or if you are going to want to handle some of the missing points, and go from there.

Chapter 13: What Else Can I Do with Python Machine Learning?

This guidebook has taken some time to look through the different algorithms and models that you can use when you work with machine learning, as well as how you can work with the Python coding language at the same time. These are a nice mixture of supervised learning, machine learning, and more to help you see results in a short amount of time.

With that said, there are even more algorithms that you can use when it comes to Python machine learning. There are so many great algorithms that are going to come with this kind of technology and coding, and they can be used in a wide variety of situations based on the kind of project that you would like to work on here. Some of the different options that you can work with when it comes to Python machine learning, in addition to the algorithms that we have already discussed in detail in this guidebook, include:

Naïve Bayes

The first method that we will talk about inside this chapter is known as the Naïve Bayes algorithm. To help us learn how this one will work, it is time to bring out a bit of imagination. To help us with this, we are going to pretend that we are in a project that has some challenges of classification. But at the same time, you want to make sure that you can come up with a new hypothesis that will work. You will also need to figure out a design that will allow you to add in new discussions and features based on how important each variable is in this model.

This may seem like it is a lot of work to do, and like we are trying to do a lot with just one type of algorithm, it is something that we can do with this option. Once you spend a bit of time collecting the information, you will probably end up with at least a few of the shareholders and other vital investors who would like to see a model of what you plan to do and produce. And often they don't want to wait until you are all done with the work to see all of this.

As a programmer, you are going to run into a dilemma here. First, the information is not all done. And even with the information that is done, you may think that the information is too complex for someone who doesn't work in data analysis to understand, especially when it is in the beginning stage. How are you supposed to make things work for your shareholders so that they know what is going on—but make a model that isn't complete—and is easy enough to help them understand what is going on? This can be hard to do.

Often when it comes to data analysis, you are going to have thousands of points, and sometimes hundreds of thousands of points, that you are going to need to show up on your model. There could even be some new variables that show up as you are working through the training and the testing. With all of this information going on—and being in the testing stage—how are you able to take this information and present it to the shareholders quickly and in a way that is easy for them to understand what is going on?

The good thing to remember here is that there is a nice algorithm, the Naïve Bayes, that will work and help you during this early stage of the model. It is designed to present all of the information that you need, while still keeping things simple enough for anyone, even someone who isn't a data scientist, to understand.

The Naïve Bayes model is meant to be easy for you to put together, and it is sometimes used to help you get through extensive sets of data in a way that is simplified. One of the advantages of working with this model is that though it is simple, it is sometimes better to work with compared to the other, more sophisticated models that you can work with.

As you learn more about how to work with this algorithm, you will start to find that there are more and more reasons for you to work with it. This model is really easy to use, especially if you are a beginner to the world of deep learning and machine learning. You will also find that it can be effective when it is time to make some predictions for our data sets and what class they should end up in. This makes it easier for you to keep things as simple as possible during the whole process. Even though the Naïve Bayes algorithm is really simple to work with, you will find that it can perform well. When compared to some of the higher-class algorithms that are out there, and some of the ones that seem to be more sophisticated, this one is going to perform the best.

However, even though there are a lot of benefits that come with the Naïve Bayes method, you need to be careful because there are a few negatives that come with it. The first negative is that when you work with an algorithm that is set with categorical variables, you need to make sure that the data you are testing hasn't already gone through a data set for training. You may find that this algorithm is going to run into some issues when it comes to making accurate predictions, and often the data sets that it assigns information to will be based more on probability than anything else.

There are several different options that you can work with that are going to make this process a bit easier and will help to solve the issues that show up here, it is sometimes a bit confusing for a beginner who hasn't been able to explore and work with machine learning. Of course, there are a lot of things to enjoy about the Naïve Bayes algorithm, but there are some drawbacks that you need to be aware of.

Remember, the Naïve Bayes is going to be able to help you do a lot of things when it comes to your presentation, but it is pretty simple. It is used as a way to show the shareholders the information that you want to present to them, but it isn't going to be able to compare the information, and it isn't able to provide the predictions that you would like—or be able to get— with some of the other options.

Working with a Regression Algorithm

While working with the Naïve Bayes algorithm is a great option to go with, another algorithm that you may be interested in is going to be known as the regression analysis. This is a type of algorithm that is going to be the one you want to look at when you would like to see if some relationships are showing between your predictor and dependent variables.

Programmers will see how this technique works well when they want to check out whether there is a casual relationship that shows up between the forecasting, with the different variables they want to work with, or even the time series modeling that you have in place. The point of working with this algorithm is that it will help you to grab all of the information found in your data set and then try to get it to fit onto a curve or a line, at least as much as possible. Of course, depending on the type of data points that you are working with, it may not work out the way that you will plan. But it is an excellent place to start, and it will help you to see if there are any commonalities between the points of data that you have.

Many times, a company will choose to work with this kind of algorithm because it helps them when it is time to make predictions. The company will then use these predictions to increase their overall profits. In some cases, you can use it to help you estimate how much the sales of a company are going to grow, while still being able to base it on the conditions of the economy right now.

One thing that a lot of data scientists like about this one is that they can add in pertinent information that they want to use. You can add in any information that is going to help you get started with this regression algorithm, including current and past economic information. This will be used inside the learning algorithm to help you figure out how the company is likely to grow in the future. To make this one work the way that you need, you have to make sure that the company inputs the right information to give them the right prediction.

One example of this is that a company can use this kind of machine learning algorithm to figure out if the company is not only growing, but also if it is growing at a similar rate, or faster or slower, compared to other companies in the same industry. This information can then be used to help you to make some predictions for how the company is going to do in the future, and they can then look for some options that will help them to do better if that is needed.

There are a few different algorithms that you can use that are considered regressions, and you have to know your data, and what you want to do with it, to help you figure out which one of those regression algorithms you would like to go with. While there are a lot of different options, the most common of the algorithms of regression that you can use with this include:

- Linear regression

- Polynomial regression

- Logistic regression

- Ridge regression

- Stepwise regression

As you can see, working with the regression algorithms are going to have a few different benefits that come with them. To start, you will see that these algorithms make it easy for anyone using the information to see what relationship is present, if any, between the dependent variables and the independent variables. This algorithm is also able to show what kind of impact will happen if you try to add in a new variable or change up another kind of variable that is in your data set.

Even though there are several benefits to this method, there are a few things to avoid when working on the regression algorithm. The biggest shortcoming that you will quickly notice is that you aren't able to use this algorithm to help out with any classification problem that comes up. The reason that classification problems and the regression algorithm don't always work together is that this particular algorithm tries to overfit the data many times. So, if you do try to add in different constraints here, you will find that the whole process is going to get tedious pretty quickly.

Clustering Algorithms

While we did stop and look at a few of the ideas behind clustering earlier in this guidebook, we also need to explore this a bit more and look at the different clustering options that a machine learning programmer has available, and even more about how these clustering options are going to benefit you when sorting through the data. These algorithms are going to fit in with unsupervised machine learning—you will be able to use them in a way that helps the program learn things all on its own.

Any time that you decide to work with a clustering algorithm, you need to make sure that the data is set up in a way that is simple and easy for the computer or the system to work with. This kind of method is going to take care of some of the data that you present to it, and then make sure that the clusters will come together right.

To work with this one, before you even decide to turn on the program, you will have a nice benefit of picking out how many clusters you would like to have present. You should aim to have at least two clusters, but often there is going to be more based on the amount of information that you have present for you. These clusters are then going to be able to hold onto the information that is found in your data set. The number of clusters will relate directly to how much data you are trying to sort through, and the kind of information that you would like to get when this algorithm is done.

For example, if your goal is to take a look at your data and sort out the information that you have for male customers and the data that you have for female customers, you may be fine with having just two clusters. But if you are interested in learning more about the different age groups of your customers, then you may want to divide it up between more than those two clusters. Once you have told the algorithm how many clusters you would like to work with, it will take all of your data points and divide them up amongst the clusters that fit them the best.

The nice thing that a programmer will like about this kind of algorithm is that it will take on the responsibility of doing a lot of the work for you. This is because even though you have to figure out the clusters, the algorithm will go through and fit the data points into the clusters that you chose. To keep things organized here, we are going to call all of the main clusters that you picked out in the beginning (such as the cluster for male and the cluster for female) the cluster centroids.

So, any time that you are looking at one of the clusters, and you notice that there are quite a few points that fall inside of it, it is safe to assume that those data points are going to be similar in one way or another. There is going to be some attribute (and that attribute will vary based on the kind of cluster that you created and the data points that are inside) that show that they each are the same in some way.

Once you have been able to form up these original clusters, you are then able to take each of these and divide them up into some more sets of clusters if this works for your goals. This is often done to help dive deeper into the information, and to learn more about the customers, or the data, as possible. You can do this, dividing up the clusters as many times as you would like to gain the knowledge and insights that you are looking for here.

There are a few reasons that programmers and data scientists like to work with one of these clustering algorithms when they are doing some machine learning. The first reason is that the computation that you do thanks to the algorithms of clustering can be easy to use, are efficient when it comes to costs compared to some of the other machine learning algorithms, and you will enjoy the depth of knowledge that you can get with this. If you want to work on some challenges that come with classification, then using one of the algorithms for clustering is going to be the easiest and the most efficient way to look at this information and to get the work done.

With all of the benefits that we have talked about, you do need to use a bit of caution with this one. These clustering algorithms are going to be useful, but you have to read through the information to make predictions about where to take your company next. This algorithm is not set up to make the predictions for you. And if you are not able to set up the centroids or the clusters in the proper manner, it is possible that you are not going to get the project to work the way that you would like, and you will make the wrong predictions.

Working with the Markov Algorithm

The next algorithm we are going to take a look at is going to fit into the category of unsupervised machine learning. This is known as the Markov algorithm. This is an excellent algorithm to work with because it is going to gather all of the chosen data that you place into it and then tries to translate it in a way that can work with any coding language that you choose. This may work with the Python coding language if that is your choice, but you can pick one of the other coding languages of your choice.

One thing that you will like with this algorithm is that the computer programmer can choose the rules that are going to go with it ahead of time so that the algorithm will take the direction that you wish it to. Many computer programmers are going to work with this algorithm because they can come up with the rules, rather than being forced to use the rules that are handed to them. You can use this benefit to take a whole string of data and make sure that it is useful to the job or the project that you are working about.

Another thing that you may like about this Markov algorithm is that you can work with it in several ways, rather than being stuck with just one method. One option to consider here is that this algorithm works well with things like DNA. For example, you could take the DNA sequence of someone, and then use this algorithm to translate the information that is inside that sequence into some numerical values. This can often make it easier for programmers, doctors, and scientists and more to know what information is present, and to make better predictions into the future. When you are working with programmer and computers, you will find that the numerical data is going to be much easier to sort through than other options of looking through DNA.

A good reason why you would need to use the Markov algorithm is that it is great at learning problems when you already know the input you want to use, but you are not sure about the parameters. This algorithm is going to be able to find insights that are inside of the information. In some cases, these insights are hidden, and this makes it hard for the other algorithms we have discussed to find them.

There are still some downfalls to working with the Markov algorithm. This one can sometimes be difficult to work with because you do need to manually go through and create a new rule any time that you want to bring in a new programming language. If you only want to work with one type of programming language on your project, then this is not going to be a big deal. But many times, your program will need to work with several different languages, and going in and making the new rules a bunch of times can get tedious.

What Is Q-Learning?

We haven't spent a lot of time taking a look at what is known as reinforced machine learning in this guidebook. But they can be incredibly useful when you are working with the ideas of machine learning in your projects as well. And the first type of reinforced learning that we are going to take a look at here is known as Q-learning. With this algorithm, you will be able to use it along with a project that needs temporal difference learning. As you go through some of your learning types in machine learning, you may notice that this one is what programmers may call an off-policy kind of algorithm. It is known as this because it isn't able to go through and learn the action value function that you would get with other options.

This kind of algorithm is useful since a computer programmer can use it regardless of the kind of function they want to be able to create with their set of data, you have to take the time to go through this method and list out the specifications that you need. This is important to ensure that the learner or the user will pick out the right course of action that you would like. This does add in a few more steps to the model compared to some of the other methods that you use, which is a drawback to consider. But, because of the efficiency that comes with this model and how well it works, it is often worth the effort and the time to do these steps.

After you have been able to go through with this algorithm and find the action value function that will work the best for your data points, it is time for you to create what is going to be known as the optimal policy. How are we supposed to be able to construct this with the Q-learning algorithm? The best way to get started with this is to use the actions that you think will come in at the highest value, regardless of the state that has been chosen to do this one in.

Depending on the kind of data that you want to go through, and the results that you are hoping to get, there could be several great advantages that come with using the algorithm in machine learning for Q-learning. One of the benefits of this is that you won't have to go through all of the effort or the time that is needed to put in the models of the environment so that the system can compare the means. You will be able to compare a few, and often a lot, of actions together and compare how they are going to be together. Also, you can use any environment that you would like to with this one, and still get the same results and be able to make the predictions that you would like.

Of course, there is a negative that can come with this one. The main issue is that you will need to go through a few more steps to make this kind of learning happen. This process, because you have to write out the rules that you want to use, and write out the course of action that makes sense for your goals, there are a few more steps compared to some of the other algorithms that we talked about in this guidebook. If you are in a hurry and don't care about having specific rules in place, then this is not that big of a deal.

As we have taken the time to explore in this guidebook, there are a lot of things that you can do when it comes to working with machine learning, especially when you can implement the Python coding language with it. We have looked at a lot of the different algorithms that you can bring up that utilize both, and even some of the Python codes that you are able to use along with each one to help you see the best results.

Whether you are working with supervised machine learning, unsupervised machine learning, or reinforcement machine learning, the Python code can help you get these various algorithms up and running. This ensures that you can make predictions, figure out the right course of action, create some great programs, and so much more—with the help of machine learning. Moreover, these final few algorithms discussed in this chapter will be able to help you get even more out of the whole process of machine learning.

Conclusion

Thank you for making it through to the end of *Python Machine Learning*! Let's hope it was informative and able to provide you with all of the tools you need to achieve your goals—whatever they may be.

The next step is to start using some of the different techniques and tools that we can work through to utilize Python Machine Learning. The field of machine learning is growing like crazy. Many computer programmers are interested in learning more about how this works, as well as how they can use it, to see the best results and to help them create new technology into the future. Think of it—a few years ago, there were no such things as the Alexa device (and other similar software from other companies) that could listen to your commands and respond—and that is all thanks to machine learning!

In this guidebook, we didn't just take a look at machine learning—we also looked at how the Python coding language can be used to make this all come to fruition for us. Python, as we explored in this guidebook, is a powerful yet easy programming language that we can work with—and when it is combined with machine learning, you are going to be able to get some of the best results possible.

This guidebook took some time to look at both the Python language and machine learning, as well as some of the different algorithms that you will be able to use with both of these. By the time you get to this point, you should be well-versed in some of the different algorithms that you can work with, as well as how they are going to benefit you based on the machine learning project you would like to work with!

When you are ready to learn more about how the Python coding language and machine learning work together and when you want to learn how to make Python machine learning work for your needs, then make sure to check out this guidebook to help you get started!

Python Programming

The Crash Course To Learn How To Master Python Coding Language With PRACTICAL Exercises To APPLY Theory And Some TIPS And TRICKS To Learn Faster Computer Programming

JOSEPH MINING

Introduction

The following chapters will discuss everything that you need to know to get started with the Python coding language. There are different coding languages that you can work with. Some of them are going to be easier to work with, and some are harder and are only recommended if you are someone who codes regularly. However, when it comes to the Python coding language, even someone who has never done a bit of coding in their lives can benefit and learn all about it.

This guidebook is going to dive right into a lot of the neat things that you can do with the Python language. Whether you just want to learn a bit more about coding, enhance some of the skills that are needed in other coding languages and add to your portfolio, or have some neat ideas for an application or program that you would like to develop, the Python coding language is a great option for you to get started with.

This guidebook is going to start with some information on what Python is all about, as well as why so many computer programmers like to choose this as their coding language. We will explore some of the benefits such as: why it is so powerful yet easy for a beginner to work with, how to install it on your system, no matter what kind of operating system you are working with. Also, some of the basic parts of the code that you should know to help you develop on some of the harder stuff later on.

The rest of this guidebook is going to focus on all of the cool things that you can implement into your codes, no matter what program you would like to develop. Some of the different topics that we are going to explore when dealing with Python coding language will include the loops, conditional statements, regular expressions, how to raise an exception, and so much more!

There are so many amazing things you can do with Python language. Even as a beginner, you are going to be impressed by how easy it is to learn this language and yet be amazed at the amount of power that comes behind all of your codes. When you are ready to learn more about the Python language, and how to use the different aspects of your codes, make sure to check out this guidebook to help you get started.

There are many books on this subject on the market—thanks again for choosing this one! Every effort was made to ensure it is full of as much useful information as possible. Please enjoy!

Chapter 1: What Is the Python Coding Language, and Why Is It So Beneficial?

There are a lot of different coding languages out there that you can work with. Each of them is going to have their benefits and a lot of neat features that come with it. But when it comes to a coding language that is easy to use, that is great for beginners, easy-to-read, lots of options, open-sourced, and still has a lot of power that comes behind it, then the Python coding language is one of the best options out there.

The Python coding language has been a favorite for a lot of people over the years. They enjoy the fact that they can learn this language and still make some fantastic codes in progress, even though they are beginners and may not have worked with this coding in the past—or any coding, for that matter.

Python is a computer user's programming language. Even as a beginner, you can learn this language quickly, but there is still a lot of power behind it, which allows you to do the codes that you want. You can make complex commercial applications, automating some housekeeping tasks for your system, or have some fun and make your games and programs.

Of course, just like with all the other programming languages, Python has a set of rules and structures that all programs need to follow. No matter what code you decide to write, it is important that you follow the rules in Python. However, compared to some of the other programming languages that are out there, you will find that this coding language is simple, compact, and very powerful. As a beginner, you will catch on quickly, and can write some of your codes in no time!

In the past, a lot of people were worried about learning a coding language. They were worried that these languages were too tough to learn, that they would get frustrated, and that only those who had spent their whole lives around computers could even attempt to write their codes—and maybe with some of the older codes, this was true.

Thanks to a lot of the newer codes introduced recently, the idea that only those gifted in computer programming could code has faded away. With many of the codes that are coming out now, including Python, anyone can learn a few of the syntaxes for what they want to do, or even find some premade codes online and make some changes. And since many of these codes are open-sourced, it is easier than ever to learn how to use them and develop the codes to meet your needs.

The modern coding languages are much better than what was found in the past with most coding languages. Gone are the days that even professionals struggled to keep bugs out of the system—and now is the time for anyone to learn how to use a coding language for their needs. This is all thanks to the development of many great object-oriented programming languages like Python.

Many coding and programming languages are available for you to choose from based on the programs and applications that you would like to create. But even with all of those different options that you have available, it is common for many computer programmers, whether they are beginners or have worked with coding in the past to choose the Python coding language.

There are a lot of reasons why people like to work with the Python code, rather than some of the other options out there. Some of the most common reasons for going with the Python language include:

There are a lot of libraries that provide you with the support you need. Just a glance through the Python environment is going to show you that many extensions and libraries will provide you with all of the help that you need to get started. You can find the classes, objects, and functions inside the language to make it easier to create all of the codes that you need. Also, it is possible to bring in some of the third party libraries from outside sources to the mix to help you get more of the features and power that you want.

Features of integration: Python is a great language to work with for many reasons, but one of these is because it can integrate with the Enterprise Application Integration. This means that you can work with some of the different Python components that it has, including COM and COBRA. There are also some control capabilities so that it can work with C, Java, and C++. It can work with many markup languages, including XML, and can use any of the modern operating systems so it will work with whatever you have when you get started.

Allows the programmer to be more productive. The Python language has a ton of different designs that are going to work here, object orientation in it, and the support libraries that you need. Thanks to all of these various resources, and the fact that it is super easy to work on this program, it is easy for the programmer to find ways to increase how productive they are. They can use this kind of productivity to help them with some of the other coding languages you want to work with as well.

It is easy to learn: The primary purpose behind this language is that it was developed to be easy to use and easy to adapt to different purposes. This makes it easy for a programmer to work with, even if they are a beginner. We are going to learn more about this language and look at some of the codes that go with Python and help you to get the most out of this language so that, even as a beginner, you can write some powerful programs.

It is easy to read through this language. As you look through some of the codes that come in this language, you will find that it is pretty easy to read through the codes, even before learning what they mean. There isn't a lot of unnecessary information that has to show up in the code, and it is all in English, so it is easy to understand the words found in it.

Python can provide you with a lot of programming power. One thing that you may be impressed with when you start on the Python language is the amount of power that is behind it. Even though this language is classified as more of a beginners' language, it is easy to adapt it and learn how to use it for any program and application. And if you learn how to combine it with some of the other high-end coding languages out there, you will see it come with even more power as well.

A big community of support Since Python is one of the biggest and most popular of all the coding languages worldwide; it has a big community of those who are learning how to use the language and those who are already well-versed in how to use it. You can take advantage of all this information and learn from it. You can ask questions, watch tutorials, or find out something new with this language as you go.

It is an open-sourced program. What this means is that you will be able to get the code for free, as well as any updates that come with it. There are some third-party add-ons that you will need to pay for if you choose to use them, but it is possible to use Python without those so you will get it all for free.

As you can see, there are a lot of great things that you are going to enjoy when you decide to get started with the Python code and use it for your own needs. Whether you are trying to add a new programming language to your arsenal to help you work well with your codes, or you are a beginner who wants to enter into the world of technology, the Python coding language is one of the best options for you to get started with.

Getting Python on Your System

Before you can utilize the information in this guidebook and write out any codes to help you develop your programs, you need first to make sure that Python is on your computer or the other system that you are using. And if it isn't there, then we need to pick out a version of Python and then download it.

Depending on your computer system, it is possible that you already have it available on your computer. Check to see if this is true. If you find that your system doesn't have this language on it, or you are not happy with the Python version that is already present on your computer, then it is time to either add it on or make the changes to a newer version.

Since Python is an open-sourced programming language, you can get everything that you need for free. If you want to add something special to the environment, or you want to have a different library, you may have to go through and add that on and pay for it. But if you want to use the basics of the Python language, as well as the great libraries and other resources with it, then you can get it for free.

With that said, there are going to be a few different available versions of Python, and choosing the one that you would like to work with the most can be a bit tricky. Since Python is going to be an interpreted language, it comes with a lot of advantages over some of the other coding languages that are out there. You will notice that one of the advantages over the others is that Python can grow and make the changes that are necessary for your computing needs. Like the applications that you can find on your computer, Python is always being developed, and these new features that come with that development can refine and change Python throughout time.

Since Python has been around for several years now, there are a few different versions of Python that have been released through that time. All of the versions have been accepted widely, but they are going to provide you with some different benefits and features over the old version. Some of the options that are available for a programmer to choose from when trying to pick a version of this coding language to work with include:

Python 2.X: There are several versions of Python 2 that you can choose from. This is one of the older versions on the market, and while it still works fine if it is the version found on your computer, it is becoming a bit dated, and many people are going to work with one of the newer Python 3 options.

Python 3: If you can choose a version to go with, then Python 3 is going to be the best option. It is the latest and includes most of the third party add-ons that you will need, the developments and features that you need for most projects, and it is going to have updates that come out. If you are choosing to download a version of Python onto your computer, then this is the best one to go with.

Installing the Interpreter on Python

Now, before you can write out any of the codes that we want to explore in this guidebook, or use the Python language at all, it is important you go through and install the interpreter. Installing this language is going to depend on the operating system that you would like to use to run this, as well as the source where you are getting the installation. There are a few different sources for downloading this language, and some are going to be more of a modified version of the code rather than the original release, so make sure that you are checking into this ahead of time as well.

From here, we are going to break up this whole process of installation and see how it behaves on the different operating systems. This makes it easier for you to get the Python language downloaded on the system that you need without any problems.

Mac OS X

The first operating system that we are going to work with is for those who are using the Mac computer. If you have this operating system, then you will find that Python 2 is going to be installed already on the computer. The exact version that comes with this will depend on the version of the operating system that you have running, and you can determine this quickly. Open up the app for the terminal and then type in the prompt: `python - V`

When you do this, the system is going to tell you what version of Python is already on here for you to use. If you are fine with using Python 2, then close out of that and move on to writing some of your codes. But it is also possible for you to install the

Python 3 version onto the computer. To check for this installation, you need to open that terminal app again, and then use the prompt "python3 -V" to help you get started.

By the default, Mac computers, and operating systems are not going to have this version of Python installed on them. If you would like to use this still, you will need to visit the python.org website and install a few of the options that are on there. This is often the best place to do your installation because it will make sure everything is added to your computer. So, once the download is done, you can open up Python and start writing the code. It is much better to have the interpreter, development tools, the IDLE, and the shell for Python already on your computer, rather than having to double check all the time and download things on their own.

Whether or not you can run the shell and the IDLE on Python are going to depend on the version that you will run on the computer, and your preferences on the matter. The commands that you can use that will bring up the applications for IDLE and the shell will include:

Type in "Idle" if you are working with a version of Python 2.
Type in "Idle3" if you are working with a version of Python 3.

Windows Systems

It is possible that you are going to want to work with the Python coding language on your Windows computer. You will not have the language automatically added to your computer because Microsoft already has its programming language present there. Python may not be standard here, but you can still go through and install it on the computer if you would like. You will also need to go through and add in the environment variables that you want because these are not done by default either. You will then be able to run any of the scripts that you need for Python going from the command prompt. The steps to get this done will include:

To set this up, you need to visit the official Python download page and grab the Windows installer. You can choose to do the latest version of Python 3, or go with another option. By default, the installer is going to provide you with the 32-bit version of Python, but you can choose to switch this to the 64-bit version if you wish. The 32-bit is often best to make sure that there aren't any compatibility issues with the older packages, but you can experiment if you wish.

Now, right click on the installer and select "Run as Administrator." There are going to be two options to choose from. You will want to pick out "Customize Installation."

On the following screen, make sure all of the boxes under "Optional Features" are clicked and then click to move on.

While under Advanced Options," you should pick out the location where you want Python to be installed. Click on Install. Give it some time to finish, and then close the installer. Next, set the PATH variable for the system so that it includes directories that will consist of packages and other components that you will need later. To do this, use the following instructions:

Open up the Control Panel. Do this by clicking on the taskbar and typing in Control Panel. Click on the icon.

Inside the Control Panel, search for Environment. Then click on Edit the System Environment Variables. From here, you can click on the button for Environment Variables.

Go to the section for User Variables. You can either edit the PATH variable that is there or create one.

If there isn't a variable for PATH on the system, then create one by clicking on New. Make a name for the PATH variable, and add in the directories that you want. Click on close all the control Panel dialogs and move on.

Now, you can open up your command prompt. Do this by clicking on Start Menu, then Windows System, and then Command Prompt. Type in "`python`." This is going to load up the Python interpreter for you.

When you get to this point, the program is going to be all set up and easy to use on the Windows system. You can open up the interpreter when you are ready, as well as everything else that is needed and can work on writing out codes and creating the programs that you would like.

Linux System

And the final step that we will need to follow to get this coding language and all of its environment set up on your computer is to look at the steps that you can take for this on a Linux computer. As more and more computer programmers are moving to use the Linux system to help them get their work done and work with coding. It is always a good idea to learn how to make this work on this kind of operating system as well.

The very first step that we need to take is to check and see which version of Python is already on the system and check if Python 3 is already there. To check on this, you need to open up the command prompt on your computer and work with the following code inside:

```
$ python3 - - version
```

If you are on Ubuntu 16.10 or newer, then it is a simple process to install Python 3.6. You need to use the following commands:

```
$ sudo apt-get update
$ sudo apt-get install Python3.6
```

If you are relying on an older version or Ubuntu or another version, then you may want to work with the *deadsnakes* PPA, or another tool to help you download the Python 3.6 version. The code to do this includes:

```
$ sudo apt-get install software-properties-common
$ sudo add-apt repository ppa:deadsnakes/ppa
# sudo apt-get update
$ sudo apt-get install python3.6
```

One thing that you may note here is that if you are working with some of the other distributions that are available through this operating system, it is very likely that the whole program of Python 3 will be found on the system already. If not, you can use the package manager of the system to help. If you notice that the version of Python 3 is not the right one or not recent enough, for your needs, you can then use the same steps to make sure that a newer version of Python gets installed the way that you would like.

Working with the Python Interpreter

If you go through and do the standard installation through the Python program through python.org, then the work is going to be done for you here. It is going to contain all of the licensing and information and documentation that you need, along with the three files that are imperative to helping you develop and run all of the scripts that you need on system. These three files are going to include the shell, interpreter, and IDLE for Python.

First, we need to take a look at the interpreter. This is an important piece to the puzzle that you need to have in place because it is the part that will execute any of the scripts that you want to write in this language. The interpreter is then able to convert the .py script files into instructions, and can then go through and process them based on the file type and the code type that you decide to write in there.

Next, you are going to notice the IDLE of this language. IDLE is going to stand for the integrated development and learning environment. It will have all of the tools that you need to help develop programs in Python. You will find many tools in here including those for debugging, for the text editor, and the shell of the language.

Depending on which version you choose to go with on Python, you may find that the IDLE is either pretty basic or extensive and full. If you are looking through the IDLE that comes with Python, and you don't care for it, or you have done some research and have found a different version of the IDLE that you would like to work on better, you can download that in as well. Often, most people are okay with the IDLE, but they will choose to go with a different text editor to get more of the features that they want. But you can certainly stick with the text editor and IDLE that are present with Python and make some fantastic codes and programs in the process.

And finally, we are to the Python Shell. This is an important thing that you need to make sure gets downloaded on your computer because it is the interface that is part of the command line and very interactive, which works with the interpreter. This is the part that will hold onto any of the codes and the commands that you write out. If the shell can look at what you are writing and understands it, then it can execute the code, and the information that you want will show up on the screen. However, if you don't write the code correctly, or the shell isn't working correctly, then there are going to be problems with the code doing what you want.

All three of these components, as well as any of the other features that you need for your programming, can be essential to ensure that you can get the most out of writing your code. If you decide to go through python.org to download this information on any of your operating systems, then all three of those components are going to be downloaded and installed for you, making the work easier, and letting you get to work writing your codes in no time.

There are times, though, when the individual will choose to go outside of the python.org to get the version of Python that they want. This is fine if you decide to do that, but you do need to double-check the files that you are getting and see if those three main components are present in there or not. If they aren't, then make sure that you find each of them and that you will get them installed on your computer as well. Forgetting to do this, or just deciding not to, is going to guarantee that your codes are not going to work the way you want. So, you may as well get them done now rather than being frustrated later on.

Chapter 2: The Basics You Need to Know About the Python Code

Now that we have taken the time to learn a bit more about Python learning and all of the neat things that you can do with it, it is time to look a bit more in depth when it comes to the different parts that are available with Python. There are a lot of necessary parts that are going to show up in almost every code that you decide to write. You will notice that there are keywords that tell the program how to run. You will see that there are functions and identifiers, and a lot of other parts of the code that are super important.

As a beginner, it is a good idea to get a handle on these different parts so that you can get the best results overall. These will make it easier to work with some of the other parts that we talk about, and will ensure you can write out codes that suit your needs. Some of the basics that show up in the Python codes you will write include:

The Keywords

The first thing that we need to look at here is the keywords. These seem pretty simple, but it is so important to understand that they tell the compiler how it needs to act and behave with the projects that you are doing. These keywords are ones that are reserved to tell the compiler what it needs to do. Since they are reserved, the computer programmer needs to remember to use them properly so that the compiler can take that command and get things done.

You need only to use them in the specified parts of the code, or it leads to error messages and other problems. If you properly use them, the compiler will be given command of what you want it to do, and it can then execute the code in the right way. These words are essential to the whole code, and learning what they are is going to make code writing easier as well. You will be able to notice a lot of these keywords as we progress through this guidebook and write some of our codes.

The Importance of the Identifiers

The next thing that you need to learn about when you are writing your codes is the identifiers. These identifiers are going to come in handy when you are writing out codes in Python, and there are a number of these that you can work with. You will find that they do have a few names to them, and you may see them through this guidebook as variables, functions, classes, and functions—to name a few.

The good news here is that even though all of them have different names attached to them, and work in different ways in the code, they are still going to have the same rules when it is time to label and name them. This can make it a lot easier to remember the rules, ensuring that you do it correctly and that the information can be called out when the code needs it the most.

So, when naming these identifiers, the first rule that you have to keep in mind is how to name these. There are a lot of options that you can work with when it is time to name one of these identifiers. For example, you can use the underscore symbol, any number, and both lowercase and uppercase letters to get this all done. You can do any combination of this that you would like to name the identifier that you are using properly.

However, you have to remember that there is an order that needs to happen with these, or they are not going to react the way that you would like. First, you are not able to start the name of this identifier with a number. You also do not want to leave any spaces if you are using more than one word to name the identifier. So, you cannot write out the name of an identifier as "3 kids" or "three kids," but you could do "threekids" or "three_kids," and it would save right. If you try to go against any of these rules, you will see that the compiler will bring up an error signal for you.

When you are trying to pick out the name that you would like to give your identifier, you can easily pick from the rules above and also remember that you need to pick out a name that you can remember that makes sense for that part of the code. If you are writing out the code and you named an identifier something that you cannot remember or difficult, then you will run into trouble adding it in later on. But outside of those few rules, you can give your identifier any name that you would like.

Working with the Control Flow

Another topic that we need to explore when we are working in the Python language is known as the control flow. This is important because it has been set up in a way to make sure that all codes you write in Python are going to be done in the right way, and that the compiler will be able to read them.

There are a few strings that you may try to use in the code, and you need to make sure that all of the parts are in the right place at the right time, or the compiler is going to run into trouble reading them. The good news is that the control flow in Python is going to be pretty easy to work with, and you can catch on to some of the rules, and how they work in Python by glancing through a few of the codes that are present throughout this guidebook.

The Statements

Statements are a pretty easy thing to catch, but we are going to take a moment to bring them up and help you understand the best way to work with them. When we are talking about statements in this language, we are talking about the string of code that the computer programmer is going to write out, and then have the compiler list it out on the computer screen.

Any time that you tell the compiler a set of instructions that you would like to work on, you will find that these are going to be the statements that you are working on in the code as well. As long as these statements are written out in the right way, the compiler is going to read them, and then give you a message, the message sent out ahead of time on the screen. The statements can be as long or as short as you would like, as long as you make them work with the code that you are writing.

The Comments

As you go through and write some of your codes, you may quickly notice that it is important to add in a little reminder or a little note. This could be a kind of explanation for what you are doing in this specific part of the code. These are little notes that you would put in place because they remind you, and tell other programmers who are going through the code, what is going on at a particular part of it. It can also add some organization to the code as a whole.

The nice thing about working with these comments is that you can add them in, and with the right things in place (namely the # in front of the comment), the compiler will choose to skip right over the comment and continue with other parts of the code. This saves you time and ensures that you can add in the explanations and the notes that you want to the code without having to worry about how it will affect the code at all.

You can work through your code and write in as many of these comments as you would like. Just make sure that the comments are useful and belong there. You don't want to waste anyone's time with these comments to clutter things up and not make the whole thing look nice at all. Having too many comments is not a good thing. But if you think that your project needs it to help explain something, then go ahead and add some more in as well.

The Variables

The next thing that we are going to work on here are the variables. These are important to the Python code because you are going to find them pretty often in any code that you decide to work on. The variables are there because they can help store some of the different values that you are trying to add to the code. And when you assign a value to one of your variables, it keeps things organized and looking nice.

You can add in any value that you want to the variable, make sure that the equal sign is present so that the compiler knows where that value is meant to go. And, if you properly do the process, you can even go through and make more than one value attach to the same variable. This is done in some of the more complex codes that you may choose to work with, but it is still something that you may want to do on occasion. You need to add in the equal sign between each part to show the compiler that one variable is going to take care of more than one value at the same time.

Classes and Objects

Other topics that we can look at are the classes and the objects. Since Python is considered an object-oriented language, it is going to divide things up into classes and objects, to make it a bit easier to work with. This ensures that you can find the information that you need in the code, without a lot of hassle or worry about where it will go.

A good way to think about the classes and objects is like having a box. Each box is going to be your class, and it is responsible for holding onto certain objects. You can put as many objects inside each class as you would like, but you need to make sure that they go together in some manner. When someone takes a look in that class, it needs to make sense why they would see certain items in that class, and why certain items should be left out.

Now, the items in a class don't need to be the same, nor should you try to make them this way. But they do need to have some relation to one another and make sense for why they are in the same class as each other. Maybe you have a class of vehicles; you can put all the cars, trucks, vans, and more in there because they are all a type of vehicle for example,

This is a better way to split up the information and the data that you want to store on Python. It ensures that when you call up one of the objects that you saved, it is going to show up in the code where it is supposed to. Without this, you could run into some issues as things get lost, and it makes things more confusing for someone who is a beginner.

The Operators

The final part of the Python code that we are going to explore here is the operators. These are a great thing to learn how to work with, and even though they are simple, they are going to add a lot of power to the codes that you are doing. When you start going through your code, you will see that there are many types of operators that you can work within your code. For example, you may work with the arithmetic functions to help you any time you want to multiply, subtract, divide, and add your parts together. There are also the assignment operators that give value over to the variable, the comparison operators that will look at your different codes and determine if they go together or are similar or not and more.

Learning these operators can make writing any code that you have a lot easier. They will do comparisons, math, and assign the values that you need. And often, they use basic symbols to help get the work done. As you look through some of the codes that are going to be present throughout this guidebook, and even some of the other topics that we will talk about, you will notice a lot of these operators tend to show up, and if they weren't present, it could cause some issues with how well the code would work.

These are some of the basic parts that come with a code you would need to write in the Python language. You will need to learn how each of these works to write some of the basic codes that come with this language and make sure that you can use this language to write your codes. Even when you are working on the codes that are hard and complex to do, you may find some of these basic parts are inside as well!

Chapter 3: Working with Conditional Statements

Now, it is time to move on to the topic of conditional statements, which can also go by the name of decision control statements. These are going to be the statements that allow the computer to make some decisions, based on the input that the user has, as well as what you would like to happen with the program. You will have many times in your program where you will want the computer to make some decisions and complete itself when you are not there. If you are working on a code where you would like the user to put in their answer, rather than giving them two options to work with, then these decision control statements are going to be good options to work with.

There are going to be a few different options that you can work with when you are making these conditional statements. The three most common ones are going to include the if statement, the if else statement, and the elif statement. As a beginner, we are going to start with the basics of the if statement to get a good idea of how these can work, and then we will build up to understand some of the more complicated things that you can do with these conditional statements.

The first option that we are going to take a look at is the if statement. The if statement is going to work with the ideas and the answer that your user gives to the computer is going to be either true or false. If the user does an input of information that is seen as true based on your code, then the interpreter can continue with the program, and it will show up the statements or the information that you would like. But, if the user is on the program and puts in something that doesn't match up with your code, and is seen as false, then the program is automatically going to end.

The good news is that we can go through a bit later, and look at the steps that you can take to ensure that you are going to get the program to respond no matter what answer your user gives, but that is not what the if statement is going to focus on. We need to take a look at this simplified form for now, and then build up from there. To help us look at how the if statement is meant to look when your user interacts with it, you will need to work with the following code:

```
age = int(input("Enter your age:"))
if (age <=18):

    print("You are not eligible for voting, try next
election!")
print("Program ends")
```

Once you have added this conditional statement to your compiler, we need to explore what is going to happen with the above code. If the user does come to this part of the program, and they say that they are under the age of 18, then there will be a message that comes up on the screen. In this case, we wrote in that the message that will come up is going to be, "You are not eligible for voting, try next election!" Then the program, because we don't have any other parts of the code here right now, is going to end. But, this brings up the question of what is going to happen with this particular code if the user does say that they are older than 18?

When a computer programmer is working with the if statement, if the user puts their age in at over 18, then nothing is going to happen. The if statement is going to be the option that you use when you only want the user to pick out the one answer that your code says is true. The user has to say that they are younger than 18 in this situation, or the program is going to be done.

As you can imagine here, this is going to cause us some problems. You most likely would want to allow your user to put in any age that works for them. Some of the users who will come to this program are going to be older than 18, and you don't want the program to end without anything there because they are older than that age range. This is going to end the program before you want it to, and it doesn't look that professional with the program that you are working with when the code ends. This is a big reason why you are not going to see the if statements all that often.

But this is where we are going to bring in the `if else` statements and use those to fix this problem. These take the idea that we were going through, the issues that we brought up, and helping us to deal with them. Let's say that you are working with the code that we had before, and you want to make sure that your program brings up a result, no matter what answer the user decides to put into the program. You can write out an if else statement so that you can get an answer for those who are under the age of 18, and then a different answer for those who are 18 and older. The code for this expands out the option that we talked about before, but here is an example that you can use.

```
age = int(input("Enter your age:"))
if (age <=18):
        print("You are not eligible for voting, try next
election!")
else
        print("Congratulations! You are eligible to vote.
Check out your local polling station to find out more
information!)
print("Program ends")
```

This code is going to be a lot more useful to your endeavors and what you want to happen in your code, and it provides you with some more options than before. And the best part is that your code is not going to end because the user puts in their age. It is going to provide them with a statement on the screen based on the age that they put into it.

This code can also be expanded out to include some more possibilities if you would like. The example above just had two options, those under the age of 18 and those above. But you can have more options if it works for your program. For example, you can split up the age ranges a bit more if you would like. Maybe you want to know who is under the age of 18, who is in their 20's, who is in their 30's, and those who are older than 40. You can use this same idea and add in some more lines to it, to help meet the needs of your program using the if else statement.

Another example that you may want to use when it comes to the if else statement is when you ask the program to pick out their favorite color. You probably do not want to go through and write out enough code to handle each color that is out there in the world, but you will leave this open so that the user can put in the information that corresponds with their favorite color.

For this code, you may choose to have a list of six colors that you write out in the code (you can have more or less for what you need), and then you will have a message that corresponds to these six colors. You may pick out the colors of yellow, orange, green, blue, purple, and red. Then, you can add in an else statement so that the user can pick out a different color. If the user decides to have white as their favorite color here, then the seventh, and the final message will come up. This final message is going to be the same for any of the colors that don't fit in with the original six.

Adding this else statement, or the `catch all`, to the end of the code can be an important thing that you need to consider. You can't possibly list out all of the different colors that your user may choose to work with. You may take the time to put in a hundred different colors (but this takes a lot of time and code, and you won't want to do this), but then the user could go with the one color that you forget. If you don't add this else statement to the end, then the program is going to be lost at how you would like it to behave here.

The else statement is nice because it is going to be the one that you can use to catch more than one result from the user, and it can catch all of the answers that you don't account for, but that the user may choose to use. If you don't add statement in the code, then your program isn't going to be sure how to behave when the user puts that answer in.

The elif Statements

The other two options of conditional statements are going to be important for a lot of the codes that you would like to work with. The if statement is a good one to learn as a beginner getting into these statements, and they will help you to mostly get a good idea of how the conditional statements are supposed to work. These if statements are going to have a basis on the idea of the answer being either true or false.

In this case, if the answer received from the user is seen as true based on the conditions that you add to the code, then the program will see this and continue on its path. But if the condition is seen to be false, then the program is not going to have anything set up, and it is going to end. This is a simple idea to work with and is a good way to learn more about the conditional statements, but for many of the codes that you want to write out in Python, it is not going to give you the results that you want.

Then we took a look at the if else statements. These took this idea a bit further, and it understood that the ideas that come with the original if statements are going to be too simple.

These `if else` statements can help us handle any answer that the user will give to the system, and ensure that the program doesn't just stop. We even took a look at an example code that shows us how these kinds of statements work.

From here, we need to spend some time working on the elif statements. This is going to handle things a bit different than what the other two did, but it is still going to be useful and can add an element of fun and something different to your code. The elif statement is going to give the user a chance to pick from a few options that you present to them. And then, the answer that the user chooses is going to provide them with a predetermined statement that you added into the code.

There are different places where you can see these conditional statements. The elif statement is a unique code for the Python language, and it is often going to be used for many games, or for a different program that you would like to have with menu style of choices for the user. These statements are going to be used most often if the computer programmer would like to provide their user with some options rather than just one or two.

When you are working with these elif statements, there is a lot of freedom in what you can do with these codes. You can add in as many statements and options as you want as long as you follow the proper coding with it. Also, you should be a bit careful with adding in too many of the options. You can technically add in as many as you would like, but sometimes, it may be too much, and you may make the code unnecessarily complicated if you are adding them in without any reason. But if it works and makes sense for your code, then you can go ahead and add in as many of these as you would like.

Now that we have spent some time talking about these elif statements and what all comes with them, it is time to look at the syntax of this conditional statement to get a better idea of how it works, and when you are most likely to use it. A good example of the syntax with the conditional elif statement will include:

```
if expression1:
statement(s)
elif expression2:
statement(s)
elif expression3:
statement(s)
else:
statement(s)
```

This is a pretty basic syntax of the elif statement, and you can add in as many of these statements as you would like. Just take that syntax and then place the right information into each part and the answer that is listed next to it. Notice that there is also an else statement at the end of this. Don't forget to add this to your code so that it can catch any answer that the user puts in that isn't listed in your elif statements.

To help you better understand how these elif statements work, and how the syntax above is going to work, let's take a look at a little game that you can create using these statements:

```
Print("Let's enjoy a Pizza! Ok, let's go inside
Pizzahut!")
print("Waiter, Please select Pizza of your choice from
the menu")
pizzachoice = int(input("Please enter your choice of
Pizza:"))
if pizzachoice == 1:
        print('I want to enjoy a pizza napoletana')
elif pizzachoice == 2:
        print('I want to enjoy a pizza rustica')
elif pizzachoice == 3:
        print('I want to enjoy a pizza capricciosa')
else:
        print("Sorry, I do not want any of the listed
pizza's, please bring a Coca Cola for me.")
```

With this example, the user will be able to look at the choices, and then choose what they would like to get from the menu. If you set this up, the corresponding statement is going to come up with the option that they use. For example, if the user would like to order a *pizza rustica,* they would click on the number 2. If they would instead go with a drink, then they can do that as well. While we were working with some examples of pizza here, you can easily use this syntax and the ideas behind it to make the menu the way that you would like and provide your user with some options as well.

There are a lot of different things that you can do when it comes to using conditional statements in your code. They provide a lot of options and a ton more power while still being easy enough for a beginner to get started with. These conditional statements are going to make it easier for you to get the program to make a decision based on the input given from the user, without the programmer having to figure out all of the possible scenarios or having to be there ahead of time.

There are a lot of times when you can use conditional statements and some of the syntaxes that we have discussed in this guidebook. Open up your compiler and practice a few of them to help you get started on the right foot with using these for your own needs and programs as well.

Chapter 4: How Do Loops Work?

Another important topic to explore when we are working with the Python coding language is the idea of the loop. These are important to a lot of the codes that you will need to write, and sometimes, they can help with those conditional statements as well. One of the best things about these loops is that they can get a lot of information into a few lines, which helps to clean up your code and makes it powerful without having to write out a lot of information.

Often, you will start to bring up these loops any time when you are writing out a code where you would like to have a particular program repeat something. Even if it is a few times, this can work as well, but you don't want to mess up the code or waste your time writing that part out a few times. While it may not seem like a big deal to write out that part of the code two or three times to get it to repeat, there could potentially be times when you want to write out the code a hundred times or more. Instead of writing out a hundred lines, or multiple lines a hundred times, you would be able to utilize these loops and get it done in just a few lines. A loop is what you need to handle this work, and you will like how easy and clean it looks.

For example, you may be working on a code, and then you get to a point where you would like to have the numbers listed out from one to ten for you. Of course, this can take up a lot of code and space if you tried to write this out each time you wanted a number listed. But with a loop, you would be able to set it to continue counting up until it reached the conditions that you set ahead of time.

This sounds like it is hard, and as a beginner, you may be worried about how you would be able to do it for yourself. These loops are going to tell your compiler that it needs to repeat the same line or lines of code over and over again until the inserted conditions are met. If you would like to get the code to count from one to ten, then you would tell the compiler that the condition is when the output is higher than ten. Don't worry about this being too confusing; we are going to show you a few examples of how this can work in a moment.

Of course, when you are writing out the loop codes, you must make sure that you put in some condition that will end the loop. Beginners can often forget to set up this condition to end the program, and then they end up in some trouble. The code will keep going through the loop, getting stuck because it doesn't know when it is supposed to stop. You must make sure that you add in a break or a condition to the code so that it knows when it should stop and move on to some of the other things that should be done in the code.

With some of the other methods of traditional coding that we have talked about, or that you may have used in the past, you would have to avoid these loops and write out each line of the code. Even if there were some parts of the code that were similar, or you were retrying the same piece of code to make a pattern show up, this is how a beginner would have to do the work to get it done. This is a tedious process that takes a lot of time, and it is hard to do.

The good news is that you can get these loops and put them to work, ensuring that you can combine a few lines of code and get the compiler to read through it again until conditions are met, rather than having you rewrite the code that many times. This means that instead of writing out potentially hundreds of lines of code, you can write out a few and have the compiler read through it again until it is done.

These loops are so important and helpful when it comes to working with the Python language, and it is well worth your time, even as a beginner, to learn how to use it properly. With that in mind, there are several types of loops that you can work with to help you make your code easier to write and save a lot of space and time when writing the code.

Each of these loops is going to be helpful and can be used in different circumstances based on what you are trying to get done in the code. The three main types of loops that we are going to explore through the rest of this guidebook include the while loop, the for loop, and the nested loop.

Working with Our while Loop

So, out of the three loops that we can work with, we will start with the while loop in the Python language. The while loop is a good choice to make if you have a predetermined number of times you would like the code to cycle through that line. You can set this up ahead of time, and ensure that the loop goes through it that many times, no more and no less.

When you use the while loop, the goal here is not to allow the code to go through the cycle as many times as it wants, or an indefinite number of times, but you do want to make sure that it goes through five, or six, or however, many times are needed. If you want the program to count from one to ten, for example, then you would set up the loop to do its work ten times. It also makes sure that the loop happens one time, and then checks the conditions before doing it again. With this option, the loop will put the number one on the screen, check the conditions, and then do number two through to ten.

This is a lot to take in and may be hard to understand. The sample code below is a good way to see what the while loop is all about and check what is going to happen when you try to write it out in your compiler

```
counter = 1
while(counter <= 3):
        principal   =   int(input("Enter   the   principal
amount:"))
        numberofyeras = int(input("Enter the number of
years:"))
        rateofinterest = float(input("Enter the rate of
interest:"))
        simpleinterest = principal * numberofyears *
rateofinterest/100
        print("Simple interest = %.2f" %simpleinterest)
        #increase the counter by 1
        counter = counter + 1
        print("You have calculated simple interest for 3
time!")
```

Before we move on, take this code and add it to your compiler and let it execute this code. You will see that when this is done, the output is going to come out in a way that the user can place any information that they want into the program. Then the program will do its computations and figure out the interest rates, as well as the final amounts based on whatever numbers the user placed into the system.

With the completed example, we can set up a loop that would go through its iterations three times. This means that the user can get the results they want before the system decides to move on. As the computer programmer, you can go through this and add in more iterations, and have the loop repeat itself more if you want it to based on what is the best option for your program.

Understanding the for Loop

There are a lot of times when you may work with the while loop that we discussed above. It is going to be a great option any time that you would like to work with a loop, and often it is the only choice that you need. But, there will be some times when this loop is not going to be quite right, and you will need to change it up a little bit. The for loop is the option that you should choose here. This is considered the traditional method for loops so that you can use it in many different situations.

When you bring out the for loop, you have to make sure that it is set up in a way that the user isn't the one that has to provide the program with information on when to stop the loop. Instead, this loop is going to be set up in a way that it goes over the iteration in the order that things show up in the statement. And then, as it reads through the statement, this information is going to show up on the screen. This can nicely work because it isn't going to need any outside force or any outside user to input information in. A good example of how this code is going to loop when you write it out includes:

```
# Measure some strings:
words = ['apple,' 'mango,' 'banana,' 'orange']
for w in words:
print(w, len(w))
```

When you work with the for above loop example, you can add it to your compiler and see what happens when it gets executed. When you do this, the four fruits that come out on your screen will show up in the exact order that you have them written out. If you would like to have them show up in a different order, you can do that, but then you need to go back to your code and rewrite them in the right order, or your chosen order. Once you have then written out in the syntax and they are ready to be executed in the code, you can't make any changes to them.

The Nested Loop

And the third type of loop that can work well when you write codes in the Python language is known as the nested loop. You will find that this one is going to work a bit different than the for, and the while loops that we did, but it can be useful in many different situations. When you decide to write out a nested loop in your code, you are taking a loop, whether it is a `for` or a `while` loop, and then placing it inside of another one. Then, the original loop and the second loop will continue to run until both are done.

This may seem like a lot of work to add in another loop to your code, but there are times when you will work on a code, and this is needed. For example, maybe you have a code that is going to include a multiplication table. It would be a lot of work and wasted time to type out all of the numbers and everything that you need for the multiplication table, getting it to go from $1*1$ up to ten times ten.

That is a lot of code to think about, and whether you are a beginner or a professional with coding languages, you won't want to go through and do all of this. The good news is that the nested loop is going to handle this for you. With the help of a nested loop, you can get all of the numbers in this multiplication chart or table to show up, and it is all going to be done in a few lines of code. The way that this is going to look will include the following:

```
#write a multiplication table from 1 to 10
For x in xrange(1, 11):
        For y in xrange(1, 11):
        Print '%d = %d' % (x, y, x*x)
```

When you got the output of this program, it is going to look similar to this:

```
1*1 = 1
1*2 = 2
1*3 = 3
1*4 = 4
```

Up to `1*10 = 2`

Then, it would move on to do the table by twos such as this:

```
2*1 =2
2*2 = 4
```

And so on until you end up with `10*10 = 100` as your final spot in the sequence.

Go ahead and put this into the compiler and see what happens. You will have four lines of code, and end up with a whole multiplication table that shows up on your program. Think of how many lines of code you would have to write out to get this table the traditional way that you did before? This table only took a few lines to accomplish, which shows how powerful and great the nested loop can be.

As you can see from the above information, these loops are going to be fantastic options that you can add into your code.

There are many reasons that you would need to add a loop into the code that you are writing, but you can quickly see how it can add a lot of information into a few lines of code, making your work faster and saving you a lot of hassle and potential mistakes along the way. Practice each of these loops a little bit so that you gain some more familiarity with how each of them works, and help you to learn when you are the most likely to use them in your code.

Chapter 5: Writing an Exception in Your Code

The next thing is how you can handle, and even raise, some of your exceptions in the code. As you work through writing some of your codes, you will find that the Python program already has a few of its exceptions that it can bring out if you or the user does something it doesn't approve of. And on top of that, there are some that the computer programmer can add into the code, to ensure that the code is going to work the way that you would like.

If the exception is considered an automatic one, then you can find it inside of your Python library. An excellent example of this one is when the user decides to divide by zero. This is something that the Python code doesn't like, and it won't allow it to happen. If the user does try to do this, then the exception from the Python library is going to show up here. If you are raising one of your exceptions, then you need to go through and tell the computer to act in that manner.

While these are important depending on the code that we want to work with, the first type that we are going to explore are the ones that the compiler will automatically recognize without you doing anything in the code. If the user does do something that will raise the exception, then the program won't let them go through. This could happen if you add in a statement that isn't right for the code, or you misspell a class so that the compiler is not able to pull it up. Or, again, it could be when you or the user are going on the program, and you try to divide something by zero. These are a few examples of the exception that the compiler is going to recognize, and will try to raise for you automatically.

As the computer programmer in Python, it is a good idea to know about the different exceptions that are going to appear in the library of Python for you. This helps because it will tell you what you need to change up in the code, and can give you a heads up about when one of these exceptions are going to turn up in the code. Some of the exceptions that the compiler may bring up for you along with their keywords include:

Finally—this is the action that you will want to use to perform cleanup actions, whether the exceptions occur or not.

Assert—this condition is going to trigger the exception inside of the code

Raise—the raise command is going to trigger an exception manually inside of the code.

Try/except—this is when you want to try out a block of code, and then it is recovered. Thanks to the exceptions that either you or the Python code raised.

Can I Raise My Exceptions in the Code?

Yes, it is perfectly acceptable to go through and raise some of your exceptions based on what you are trying to write for your program. But first, we shall look at how you can use these exceptions in any code that you try to write. When the automatic ones, the ones that the compiler is going to understand come up, you want to make sure that you are prepared, and what you can do to make sure that it is easier to understand for the user.

If you are going through on your code, and you notice that some issue shows up, or you would like to figure out why this program is doing something that seems wrong, then you may take a look at the compiler and see that it is trying to raise a new exception for you. This is because the program has had a chance to take a look at the code and is trying to figure out how you would like to fix something that shouldn't be happening.

The good news is that a lot of the issues that are going to show up with this are going to be simple and easy to fix. For example, you may try to bring out a file that you created, but you misspelled it or gave it the wrong name, either when you first named it or when you are trying to bring it back up. Since the compiler cannot find the name, it is going to raise an exception for this.

A good way to get a look at how this exception is going to work; we are going to stop here and look at an example of what it looks like when the compiler raises one of these exceptions. Add the following code into your compiler so that you can get an idea of what happens when an exception shows up in your code:

```
x = 10
y = 10
result = x/y #trying to divide by zero
print(result)
```

The output that you are going to get when you try to get the interpreter to go through this code would be:

```
>>>
Traceback (most recent call last):
        File "D: \Python34\tt.py", line 3, in <module>
        result = x/y
ZeroDivisionError: division by zero
>>>
```

When you stop and look at this example and ask it to execute, the compiler is then going to bring up a nice error message on the screen. This is because the user tried to divide things by zero. Most coding languages, including Python, are not going to allow this to happen, and so the error is going to be raised.

Now, you could leave this how it is in the code, without making changes. But when you go through and leave it this way, and the user tries to divide by zero, they are going to get a quite long and messy error message. This is going to be hard to understand and often comes with a series of letters and numbers that they are not going to understand. As the programmer, you can go through with this and make some changes so that the code explains what is wrong, and the user can then make some changes. Rather than leaving them confused when a long and messy error message shows up when they do something wrong, you can use a code like the following to help show what the user did exactly to upset the compiler at this point:

```
x = 10
y = 0
result = 0
try:
      result = x/y
      print(result)
except ZeroDivisionError:
      print("You are trying to divide by zero.")
```

With this example, the code we are adding to the compiler is going to be similar to the first example that we tried to do. But with this one, there are a few changes so that the message explains what is going on any time that the user does raise the exception that is to blame here. You can add in any message that you would like at this point, but this message has to do except trying to divide by zero.

How Do I Define My Exceptions Inside a Code?

Now, as earlier discussed, the previous examples were to show us how we can manage an exception that showed up naturally in the code itself. These are ones that the Python code is not going to allow because they don't conform to things that the code can do. We also looked at some of the steps that you can take to change up the message and personalize it to the error at hand, rather than trying to have a string of letters and numbers that don't make a lot of sense.

But we can take a step further. You can raise some exceptions in the code that are all your own. These are things that the code would normally see as just fine, but which won't work based on the program that you are creating, and some of the things that you would like the code to do. You can easily raise these exceptions in the code as well if you would like.

For example, maybe you are working on a code or a kind of game, and you decide you want to allow the user to input a few types of numbers or a certain number of chances, and that is it. This can work well with some of the games or the applications that you want to create. If the user takes up all of their turns or they are not picking the right numbers to place into space, then there needs to be an error message or an exception that is going to show up in the process.

These exceptions can be fun because they are unique to the code that you are writing. You need to take some time to write them into the code that you are working on though because, since they are your exceptions, the compiler is not going to recognize them without this, and will continue to read through the rest of the code. One way that you can write out this exception in your code would include the following:

```
class CustomException(Exception):
def_init_(self, value):
        self.parameter = value
def_str_(self):
        return repr(self.parameter)

try:
        raise CustomException("This is a CustomError!")
except CustomException as ex:
        print("Caught:", ex.parameter)
```

When you finish this particular code, you are done successfully adding in your exception. When someone does raise this exception, the message "Caught: This is a CustomError!" will come up on the screen. You can always change the message to show whatever you would like, but this was there as a placeholder to show what we are doing. Take a moment here to add this to the compiler and see what happens.

And it is as easy as that. You can go through and create any exception that you would like in your code, as long as you use the formula that is above to help you do it. You can go through and make some changes to the wording and the statements that you would like to see show up on the exceptions that you have. This can help make it more unique for your ongoing project.

Exception handling is a good topic to learn more about, and as you work to write out the more advanced codes, rather than some of the basic beginner codes that are available. There are a lot of times where you will want to either create your exceptions to the code to make your program work the way that you would like or learn how to handle some of the exceptions that the computer recognizes on its own.

Working with some of the codes that we discussed in this chapter, and spending some time adding them to the compiler and seeing what happens when you change up little things in the code can make a big difference in how quickly you can get started with this and see the results that you would like. Make sure that you practice a bit so that you are ready to work with any of the exceptions that you would like in Python, and to learn exactly how these exceptions are meant to work.

Chapter 6: Working with User-Defined Functions When You Work with Python

Functions are going to be something that many different coding languages are going to share in common. It is going to be a block of code that you can recycle to help you to work on a specific task. However, when you take some time to define one of these functions in python, you have to understand what the two main types of functions are, or you are going to run into some troubles along the way—and these two types are going to include the built-in functions and the user-defined functions.

The first kind, or the built-in functions, are going to be the ones that come with Python, the ones that are found in the libraries of this coding language. But you can define some of your functions, based on your project, and these are the user-defined functions. In Python, all of the functions will need to be treated like objects, which can often make things a lot easier to work with, as you will see in a moment.

As we go through this chapter, we will spend some time focusing on the user-defined functions and how you will be able to use these for your projects. To make this kind of concept a bit easier to work with, we are going to bring in some examples of how to work with these user-defined functions. Before we do that, though, let's look below and figure out a few of the important concepts that are needed to make more sense of these user-defined functions.

Why Are User-Defined Functions So Important?

To keep it simple, in most cases, the developer can write out a code to have their user-defined functions, or, if you are a beginner in this, you can use a third-party library that helps out with these. Sometimes, these functions are going to provide you with a distinct advantage, and some neat things that you can do, depending on the way you would like to use them up in the code. However, there are going to be some things that a developer will have to remember about these functions and the way they work in your code, including:

These functions are going to be made out of reusable code blocks. It is necessary only to write them out once, and then you can use them as many times as you need in the code. You can even take that user-defined function and use it in some of your other applications as well.

These functions can also be very useful. You can use them to help with anything you want from writing out specific logic in business to working on common utilities. You can also modify them based on your requirements to make the program work properly.

The code is often going to be friendly for developers, easy to maintain, and well-organized all at once. This means that you can support the approach for modular design.

You can write out these types of functions independently. And the tasks of your project can be distributed for rapid application development if needed.

A user-defined function that is thoughtfully and well-defined can help ease the process for the development of an application.

Now that we know a little bit more about the basics of a user-defined function, it is time to look at some of the different arguments that can come with these functions before moving on to some of the codes that you can use with this function.

Now that we have looked over these user-defined functions, it is time to take a look at the arguments of the functions that you can use. This ensures that you can get your code to do the things that you want. We will even look at some of the different codes that are available with these user-defined functions so that you end up with the results that you would like.

The Arguments of Functions Available

Any time that a computer programmer is working on a particular code in Python, these user-defined functions will be able to take on the argument of four different types. These argument types, as well as their corresponding meanings, are already defined ahead of time, and it is not something that the developer can change on their own. Instead, the developer will need to go through and follow these rules. And when they are ready, the developer can also add in a few things or take away a few things to create the customized functions that they want. There are going to be four arguments that you can use with your functions, and these will include:

The default argument: The Python coding language is going to have its way of representing the values of the default and the syntax that you are using for these kinds of arguments. These values are going to help indicate that the argument is going to take a particular value—unless you pass on a different value during the call. You will be able to tell what the default value is with the help of the equal sign.

Required arguments: These types of arguments are the ones that have to be present, the ones that are seen as mandatory for the function to work. You need to make sure that the values you are using are passed in the right order, and in the right numbers, any time that function is called out. If this doesn't happen, then the code won't work for you.

The keyword arguments: The third option of arguments that you can work with here are known as the keyword arguments. These are going to be relevant to the function calls, and they are the keywords that are going to be mentioned here, along with the values that have been assigned to them. These are the keywords that are mapped with the function arguments, which will make it easier on the programmer to identify what the right value is, even if there is a reason why the order doesn't stay where it is supposed to be. This is a good argument to use because it ensures that everything is going to stay organized in the code.

A variable number of arguments: This is another argument that you can use if you are working on a function, but you don't know exactly how many arguments need to be passed on to the function. Or you can take this one and design it in a way where the number of arguments can be passed as long as the requirements you set are met.

Writing Out Your User-Defined Functions

Now that we have spent a bit of time looking at these user-defined functions and what they are all about, it is time to learn some of the codes that need to happen inside Python to create one of your own. There are going to be four basic steps that you can follow to ensure that a user-defined function is going to appear when you are done.

Remember with this one; you have the power to make it as simple or as difficult as you would like. Of course, in this guidebook, and this chapter, we are going to look at the basics of what would need to occur to ensure your user-defined function is created. The steps that you will need to follow to make this happen includes:

Go through and declare the function. You can declare your function with the help of the "def" keyword, and then you need to have the name of the function shown up after announcing the keyword.

Now, you can write out the arguments: These arguments need to be inside the two parentheses of the function. You can then end the whole declaration with a colon so that you are following the right protocol that comes with Python.

Add in the statements that you would like the program to execute for you at this time.

And finally, you can end the function. You can decide whether you would like to go with a return statement or not with this one.

Now that we know a bit more about the steps that you can take to get your function written and ready to go with this, it is time to make one of your user-defined functions. A good example of how you would do this includes:

```
def userDefFunction (arg1, arg2, arg3, …):
      program statement1
      program statement2
      program statement3
      . . .
      Return;
```

And that is all! Follow these steps, and you can create any user-defined functions that you would like to add some power, and some uniqueness to the program that you are writing.

Chapter 7: Inheritances in the Python Code

In this chapter, we shall consider another fantastic thing that you can do in the Python coding language. This technique is called an inheritance. When you take a look at some of the codes and examples that we will provide in this chapter, it may seem a bit overwhelming at first. Some of the codes are a bit longer and look like they are complicated. The good news is that these inheritances are much easier to use than you might think, and they can take a lot of big and bulky code and make it easier to write, without having to type out a ton of lines in the process. This can ensure that the coding looks nicer, can clean up the work that you do, and still provides you with all of the results that you are looking for in your program.

So, let's get started by writing our inheritances. To help you out here, and make sure that the inheritance is going to stay as simple as possible, we first need to come up with the definition of what inheritance is all about. This inheritance is going to be when you take all or part of your original code, which is going to be called the parent code in this technique, and then copy it down and make some changes to come up with a child code.

There are a lot of things that you can do with these child codes. You can adjust them, add to them, and take away from them as you wish. This changes and adds things to this part of the code but will not affect the parent code as long as you properly did the inheritance. And you can make as many of these child inheritances, based on the original parent class, as you would like, changing and adding to each part as you would like.

As a beginner, this may sound like it is pretty complex, and is going to be hard for you to work with. But we will walk through a few examples of the codes that you can do with it, and you will find that it can be incredibly useful. You can copy down the parent code as much as you want, and then add and take away what is needed to ensure the code works how you want. To understand how this is going to work in your code, let's take a look at the following syntax and example of inheritance.

```
#Example of inheritance
#base class
class Student(object):
        def__init__(self, name, rollno):
        self.name = name
        self.rollno = rollno
#Graduate class inherits or derived from Student class
class GraduateStudent(Student):
        def__init__(self, name, rollno, graduate):
        Student__init__(self, name, rollno)
        self.graduate = graduate
```

```python
def DisplayGraduateStudent(self):
    print"Student Name:", self.name)
    print("Student Rollno:", self.rollno)
    print("Study Group:", self.graduate)

#Post Graduate class inherits from Student class
class PostGraduate(Student):
    def__init__(self, name, rollno, postgrad):
    Student__init__(self, name, rollno)
    self.postgrad = postgrad

    def DisplayPostGraduateStudent(self):
    print("Student Name:", self.name)
    print("Student Rollno:", self.rollno)
    print("Study Group:", self.postgrad)

#instantiate from Graduate and PostGraduate classes
    objGradStudent = GraduateStudent("Mainu", 1, "MS-
Mathematics")
    objPostGradStudent  =  PostGraduate("Shainu",  2,
"MS-CS")
    objPostGradStudent.DisplayPostGraduateStudent()
```

When you type this into your interpreter, you are going to get the results:

```
('Student Name:,' 'Mainu')
('Student Rollno:,' 1)
('Student Group:,' 'MSC-Mathematics')
```

```
('Student Name:,' 'Shainu')
('Student Rollno:,' 2)
('Student Group:,' 'MSC-CS')
```

The inheritance is a nice technique to learn how to work with because it adds in a lot of freedom when trying to write out a new code. If you have either a parent class or a base class that has a lot of the features that you would like to work with, or that you want to use to make the derived or the child class, then the inheritance is the way to work on this without having to rewrite the code all of those times. If you have one child class, this may not seem like that big of a deal. But if you have to do this ten, twenty, or more times in your code, it is going to save a lot of time and ensure that your program still looks nice.

It is possible that the programmer can go through and start with one parent class and create as many of the child classes as they would like. As long as they are done with one another, and you work with a syntax similar to what we have above, it is possible to add in as many of these child classes as are needed for your project.

This can make the code look nicer, can make the writing of the code easier, limit the amount that you are going to need to write out, and it ensures that you can get a new program written as quickly as possible. Each of these new derived classes can take on any of the features that it wants from that parent class, or it can even drop some of the parts if it wishes. This helps you to continue on the code, and make it work the way you would like.

Can I Override My Base Class?

Now that we have had talked about how the inheritance works with your code and some of the benefits of using inheritance, it is time to move on to the next step, which is learning how to override one of the base classes and make it work for this process.

There are going to be times when you will work with a specific derived class, and then you find that it is time to override the things that are found inside of it when you make the inheritance. When this happens, you need to do a few steps to override the actions that are found in that base class. This means that the computer programmer needs to look through their base class and change up the behavior that is found inside. This makes it easier for the derived class to get the behavior that you want and nothing else.

Don't let the idea of overriding the base class seem complicated. It is a nice way to look at the features that are in the parental class and decide which ones are going to go on to the new child class, and which ones you are going to keep behind. This also ensures that you can keep the parent class in the same place without those changes affecting it and the way your code is going to behave.

Overloading

One of the other things that a computer programmer can do when they want to work with these inheritances is a process that is called overloading. When you are working with this process, you are taking an identifier and using it to help define more than one method at the same time. Many times, this is going to be up to two methods inside each class, but you may run across a situation where it needs to define three or more in the process.

The two methods to use for this same identifier need to be inside the same class, and then the parameters need to be different for this to work. You will find that the process of overloading is going to work the best when you want to have them do a task that needs to fit with different parameters.

Overloading is not one of those processes that a beginner is going to have much use for as a beginner. But, as you work on more programs and more codes along the way, you may find more uses for it. Learning a bit about overloading and what it means can make things easier when you get started with the idea of inheritances.

A Final Note About Inheritances

As you decide to work on some inheritances inside this coding language, it is possible you will find that you can move on to multiple inheritances at the same time. When it is time to work with multiple inheritance components, you will find that as you go through each of the levels, they are all going to have similarities to one another, but you are still going through each one and making the small additions or changes that you need for each level.

With these multiple inheritances, you will notice that they are going to be pretty similar to that single inheritance that we were talking about before. But instead of stopping at just one, you will continue down through the line, adding in more things or taking away more things as you progress through the code. You will turn the derived class over to the parent class and continue through this process.

When you are working on a code, and you notice that it wants you to work with multiple inheritances to get the work done, you will need to start with one class, which is your base class, and then it will have at least two parent classes to help you out.

This is important to learn because it makes things easier when you need to borrow a few features from more than one part of the code that you have.

Multiple inheritances can be as simple or as complicated as you would like to make them. When you work on them, you can create a brand new class, which we will call Class C, and you got the information to create this new class from the previous one, or Class B. You can go back and find that Class B was the one that you created from information out of Class A. Each of these layers is going to contain some features that you like from the class ahead of it, and you can go as far as possible into it as you would like. Depending on the code that you decide to write, you could have ten or more of these classes, each level having features from the previous one to keep it going.

While creating these inheritance components, remember that you are not allowed to move from multiple inheritance components over to a circular inheritance. You can add in as many of your parent classes as needed to the code, but you can't make it go in a circle and connect things with this method.

As you start to write out some more codes inside the Python language, you will find that working with different types of inheritances can be pretty popular. There are many times when you can stick with the same block of code in the program, and then make some changes without having to waste your time rewriting the code over and over again.

Chapter 8: Working with the Python Generators

The next topic that we are going to explore a bit is going to be the Python generators. They are a type of function that is meant to help you create a sequence of results. These generators are great because they can maintain their local state, allowing the function to resume where it left off any time that it is called up more than once. You should think of this generator in a way similar to the iterator. The function state can be maintained with a simple keyword of "`Yield`." In Python, you can think of this as typing in "`return`," but we are going to explore some of the differences that come up with this.

How Does a Generator Work?

There are a lot of different things that these generators can do to help make your code as strong as possible. But the best way for a beginner to learn more about generators and how they are meant to work will be to look at an example like the one below:

```
# generator_example_1.py

Def numberGenerator(n):
    Number = 0
```

```
    While number < n:
    Yield number
    Number + = 1

myGenerator = numberGenerator(3)

print(next(myGenerator))
print(next(myGeneartor))
print(next(myGenerator))
```

The above code is going to be put into the compiler and defines the generator for you. In specific, it is going to define the generator that goes under the name of "`numberGenerator`," and it is going to provide you with a value of 'n' as the argument. This happens before you can go through all of this, and define it with the help of a while loop to help with limiting the value. Also, this is all going to go through and help when it is time to define a variable that comes with the name of "`number`," and it can then assign the zero value back to this.

Any time you want to use the `myGenerator`' to bring up an instantiated generator with the `next()` method, it is going to go through and run the generator through the whole code until you get to the 'yield' statement. For example, this is going to return 1 to you. Even when you do get the value returned in this scenario, your function is going to try and keep the variable written as 'number" when you call up the function next, but it will let the value grow by one. What this means is that this is going to start up again right where it left off, and the next time the function is going to be called up, it will continue from there.

If you were doing this and you wanted to call up your generator more than once following that code written above, then you will find that it raises an exception (remember we talked about those exceptions a bit earlier on). It is going to say "StopIteration" since the generator is done, and it has finished up and reverted out from that internal while loop it was doing.

This is a strong thing to see in the code sometimes, but the functionality is very useful because you will be able to work with these generators to help you create any of the iterable components that you would like.

The Differences in "Between" and "Yield"

Now, there are a few times when you will want to change up the keyword that you are using. Sometimes, you will need to use the return keyword. This is used when you would like to get a return of a value from the given function. And when you do use it, the function is going to get lost out of the local state.

This means that once you go back and try to call up that function for the second time, then the function got lost, and it is going to restart from the first statement.

If that is what you would like the function to do, then this is not a bit problem. But, you can also work with the yield keyword to help keep the state between the different calls of the functions. This method is helpful because it ensures that after you are doing using it, the function is going to go back from where it was first called up. This is a good one to choose depending on the place you want your function to end up when all is said and done.

How Do I Use the return in a Generator?

The generator can use the statement for 'return' but only when there isn't a `return`value. The generator will then go on as in any other function return when it reaches this statement. The return tells the program that you are done and you want it to go back to the rest of the code. Let's take a look at how you can change up the code to use these generators by adding in an if else clause so that you can discriminate against any numbers that are above 20. The code you would use for this includes:

```
# geneator_example_2.py
```

```
def numberGeneator(n):
    if n < 20:
    number = 0
    while number < n:
    yield number
    number +=1
else:
    return
print(list(numberGeneator(30)))
```

This particular example is going to show that the genitor will be an empty array. This is because we have set it so that it won't yield any values that are above 20. Since 30 is above 20, you will not get any results with this one. In this particular case, the return statement is going to work in the same way as a break statement. But, if you go through this code and you get a value that is below 20, you would then see that show up in the code.

Additional Information That You Need to Know About Generators

When you are working with these generators, you should remember that it is going to be a new type of iterator, one that the Python code has already gone through and defined with the notation of a function so that it all becomes easier to use.

When you work with these generators, you are working with a function type that is going to give you a yield expression.

Now, these are not going to get you a return value if that is what you want. However, when you use these, they are going to give you the results that you are looking for. The process to help you call out the generator is going to be considered a process that is automatic in Python. The context that you need to use is going to be the value that your local variables have, the location of the needed control flows, and other factors as well.

Now, there are some options when it comes to calling up the generator that you want to use. If you call it with the help of __next__, the yield you are going to get will show up at the next iteration value in the line. You can also choose to work with __iter__, which is one that will automatically implement in your program, and it tells the program that it should take that generator and use it in the best place where an iterator is needed.

As a programmer, there are a few options that you can choose from when it comes to working on these generators. Some of the options that you can use include:

Generator expressions: These types of expressions give you as the programmer the ability to define a generator with a simple notation. This is done when you are creating your list in Python. You would use the methods of __iter__ and __next__ because they provide you the results for any objects in the generator type.

Recursive generators: It is possible for your chosen generator to be recursive, just like what you would find with some functions. The idea here is that you would swap all of the elements that are on your list with the one on top, allowing all of them to move to the first position, and the rest of the list is then gone.

Are There Specific Times When I Should Work with a Generator?

One question that some beginners are going to have when they go through this chapter is when they should consider working with a generator in their code. As we have seen through some of the examples and the things we have talked about in this chapter, the generators can be more advanced tools that are needed to write out the code that you have. In programming with the Python language, there can be times when these generators are useful, and they can improve the efficiency of your code. Some of the scenarios about when you would need to work with these generators will include

Any time that you are working with a lot of data that needs to be processed through, generators are going to be helpful because they can calculate instantly. This is often the process used with stream processing.

You can also work with what is known as stacked generators with the pipping process. This is when you would be able to use generators to pipeline a series of operations so that things are as easy as possible in your code.

Chapter 9: What Are the Regular Expressions?

Any time you are ready to work on some codes in the Python language, one thing that you may notice about all of this is that Python comes with a great library. This Python library is going to contain a lot of the things that you need to write the code, including regular expressions, and it is going to be at least partly responsible for handling the searches you want to do while also taking care of the different coding tasks that need to happen behind the scenes.

You will be able to take and use these regular expressions in the code to help you filter out the different strings of text or individual parts of the text. It is possible to check and see if a string or some other text is already inside the code, and whether or not it is going to match up with some of the regular expressions as well. The nice thing about these regular expressions is that you can stick with a similar syntax, no matter the language you choose to go with. So, if you learn how to get this done inside the Python language, you can take the knowledge and work with regular expressions in other languages as well.

By this point, we have talked about some of the benefits of regular expressions, but we haven't explored what these expressions are all about, or even how you will be able to use these regular expressions inside your code. A good place to start for this process and help you to understand is to bring out your text editor, and then try to get the program to locate any word that was spelled in two different manners in the code. These regular expressions can be used to cut out the errors and the confusion that could come up with this problem.

You will quickly see that working with these regular expressions can open up a world of different things that you can do with the code you have on hand and are writing. This is why learning how to use these regular expressions properly is going to be so important. If you would like to bring out these expressions and start using them in your code, the first thing that you need to do is import the expression library. Do this when you first start to install Python because you are likely to use these regular expressions quite a bit.

There are a lot of different regular expressions that a computer programmer can choose from when they want to write out their statements. And if you know ahead of time how these statements work and all of the things that they can do, it is going to make a big difference on what you can make your code do. Let's spend a bit of time here looking at the regular expressions that are the most common, how these expressions work, and how you can use them properly in your code.

The Basic Patterns Present

One thing that a lot of computer programmers like about these regular expressions is that they aren't stuck with just having them present for one fixed character. These regular expressions are going to help you watch out for some of the patterns needed along the way. As you work on these regular expressions, you may notice that some of the most common patterns that show up include:

a, X, 9, < -- ordinary characters match themselves exactly. The meta-characters that aren't going to match themselves simply because they have a special meaning include: . ^ $ * ? { [ ] and more.

. (the period)—this is going to match any single except the new line symbol of '\n'

\w—this is the lowercase w that is going to match the "word" character. This can be a letter, a digit, or an underscore. Keep in mind that this is the mnemonic, and it is going to match a single word character rather than the whole word.

\b—this is the boundary between a non-word and a word.

\s—this is going to match a single white space character, including the form, tab, return, newline, and even space. If you do \S, you are talking about any character that is not a white space.

^ = start, $ = end—these are going to match to the end or the start of your string.

\t, \n, \r—these are going to stand for tab, newline, and return

\d—this is the decimal digit for all numbers between 0 and 9. Some of the older regex utilities will not support this so be careful when using it

\ --this is going to inhibit how special the character is. If you use this if you are uncertain about whether the character has some special meaning or not to ensure that it is treated like another character.

Of course, these are a sampling of the different regular expressions that you can bring out and use inside your codes. Make sure to try them out a few times because they are important, and you need to gain some experience with them to ensure they work properly in your code. There are many different instances and types of codes that will need these regular expressions, and there are even times when you will need more than one to get the results you would like in the code.

Doing Queries in Python with the Help of Regular Expressions

Now, not only are you able to use these regular expressions to help you find basic patterns in the code that you have, but it is also possible to use these as a way to search for any input string inside the code. There are going to be three methods available for you to do these searches, based on what you are trying to find in the code. Each code and each part of the code is going to require you to do a different query type to get things to work. Let's take a look at each of these three, and get a better idea of how each one does work.

The Search Method

The first query option we shall consider is the search method. This one is helpful to use because it is going to allow the programmer to match up the query, no matter where it shows up in the code to start with. This function isn't going to come with as many restrictions as the other two we will talk about. If you would like to search for a word or a few words throughout the whole string, and not just at the beginning of it or the end of the string, then the search method is the one that you will want to work with.

When you utilize this search method, it is going to help look for a word or a statement that shows up inside your string. It doesn't matter where this item shows up, even if it is the last part of the whole string. An excellent example of what this is going to look like when you type it into your compiler includes

```
import re
string = 'apple, orange, mango, orange'
match = re.search(r'orange', string)
print(match.group(0))
```

Before we move on with this one, open up your compiler and add this code in to see the output. This code is, if you did it properly, it's going to provide you with the output of "orange.' For this method, we are going to see the match show up just one time, regardless of how many times the term comes in the code. So, with this one, you technically see the word orange show up twice, but the search method is going only to bring it up once. As soon as the method can find this term the first time, it is going to stop looking and will provide you with the output.

Of course, there are most likely going to be times when you would like to get an idea of how often the term does show up in the code or that part of the code. And in a few sections, we will show you how to make this happen. But for this part, you will only be able to pull up the word the first time that it is found by this method.

The Match Method

While there are some times when you will be able to work with the search method, and you will quickly see that there are a lot of things that it can do for your code, it isn't necessarily going to work with ever search and query that you would like to do. Another option that you can work with is the match method. This method is meant to help you find matches to the query, but they are only going to show up if that query item shows up at the beginning of your string. This method works well when you want it to find some specific patterns that may show up in the syntax that you would like to search through.

Looking at the example of code that we have above, you will be able to see how the match method is different compared to the search method. You can see that there is some pattern in that code, where the object of orange is going to show up between all of the words. But if you switch out the `re_search` for the re-match, then you are not going to get any results at all because orange is not the first term in that string.

Even though there is the object of orange found not only once, but twice, inside your code, it is not the first object that shows up in the string. The match method is just going to take a look at that first object that appears in the string. And since that is not going to be orange, then there is no match for you to see here.

Now, this is why it is so important to have your pattern in the right order right from the beginning. If the order is off, then you are not going to end up with the right answers here. You can change the pattern up any way that you would like when writing out the code. But once you get the code up and running, that pattern is going to stay put, and you aren't able to go through this and make any changes. With this example, with the patterns that we have is not going to have the orange show up first and with the match method, you will not get any result at all.

The Fidall Method

And the third method that we are going to work with here is going to be the final method. This is the option and search method that you will want to use when it is time to figure out how many instances of a particular object are found in a string. With the other methods that we have talked about, you are finding out if the object is found at all, or finding out if it is present as the first search item. But when you work with the final method, you are going to find out just how many oranges are present in that string. Using the code example that we had before, you are going to be able to replace it with the findall method and get the output of "orange, orange' since there are two oranges in the string.

Now, when you write out your code, you can have as many of the one object in the string as you would like. You could go through and have twenty oranges present in the string if you would like, and the findall is going to be able to put twenty oranges at the output. You can, of course, choose to work with a different object as well.

As you can see here, the findall method is a bit different compared to that search method that we talked about earlier in this chapter. Since they are a bit different, type the code into your compiler and experiment a bit with these three methods to see what outputs you can get with them as you make the necessary changes.

Working with these methods will make a big difference in the kind of searches that you can do with your code and the results that you can get with each one. Take some time to look through these and change up the code a bit to get some practice, and to see what each one can do for you.

Chapter 10: The Classes and the Objects in Python

Python is a language that is considered an OOP language, or an Object-Oriented Programming language. This may sound complicated, but it is going to mean that Python is designed in a way to make things much easier for the beginner to handle as they write their codes. The classes and the objects that are used for this language are set up to work together—ensuring that all of the information you write out in the code is going to stay where you put it and that everything maintains its organization.

To make things as simple as we can here, the classes that we will explore can be thought of as containers that are going to place all of the objects together inside. You can create as many of these containers as you would like, and then you go through and pick which objects will go into each class, based on what they have in common, and whether or not it makes sense for them to be in the same class or not. If the objects are found in the same class, then they are going to be pulled up at the same time when the code asks for them, helping to maintain the organization that we just talked about.

As a programmer working with the Python language, you will be able to make the objects that fit into an individual class what you would like, and there isn't a limit on how many objects can go into each class. With that in mind, you do need to make sure that the objects found in the same class are similar to one another. This makes your organization a bit easier and helps you to get the code to work a bit more efficiently for your needs.

Keep in mind here that just because the objects should be similar doesn't mean that they need to all be the same. However, if you or another programmer look at the classes, the objects that are inside should make sense, and they should be able to figure out how all of these objects are related.

The good thing here is that there are a lot of things that you will be able to do with these classes and these objects. But before we learn how to create some of our classes and place the objects that we want inside, we need to understand a few of the big differences between the classes and the objects. These key items include:

The objects that go into the same class need to have some similarities to one another. If someone looked into that class, it shouldn't be too hard for them to figure out how all of these items are related to each other. That doesn't mean that the items need to be identical, though. You could have a class that is labeled as fruits. You can then add in items like grapes, bananas, peaches, apples, and pears if you would like.

Classes: It is a good idea to learn about classes when you want to create a code in Python. Classes are the blueprint and the design for the objects because they will be there to tell the interpreter the right way to run your program.

Creating Your First Class

Now that we have a little bit of an understanding of what objects and classes are in the Python language, it is time to take this a step further and look at how you can create these classes. Despite how it may sound, this is a simple process to work with, as long as you make sure you are using the right syntax to put it all together.

To help you with creating your first class, you need to make sure that each class is getting a new definition created for it at the same time. When you are working on these classes, you need to have the keyword, and then right after that, you need to have the name that you want to give the class. Then, in the parentheses that follow, you need to have the superclass inside. Add in a colon at the end. Your program will still run if this part is missed out on, but it is considered good coding practices and makes it easier to read your code if you have that in there.

To help get rid of some of the confusion that can often happen with this syntax, we have a great example of how you would write out the code to create your Python class:

```python
class Vehicle(object):
#constructor
def_init_(self, steering, wheels, clutch, breaks,
gears):
self._steering = steering
self._wheels = wheels
self._clutch = clutch
self._breaks =breaks
self._gears = gears
#destructor
def_del_(self):
        print("This is destructor....")

#member functions or methods
def Display_Vehicle(self):
    print('Steering:' , self._steering)
    print('Wheels:', self._wheels)
    print('Clutch:', self._clutch)
    print('Breaks:', self._breaks)
    print('Gears:', self._gears)
#instantiate a vehicle option
myGenericVehicle = Vehicle('Power Steering', 4, 'Super
Clutch', 'Disk Breaks', 5)
myGenericVehicle.Display_Vehicle()
```

The output that you are going to be able to get from putting all of this information into your interpreter includes:

```
('Steering:,' 'Power Steering')
('Wheels:,' 4)
('Clutch:'. 'Super Clutch')
('Breaks:,' 'Disk Breaks')
('Gears:,' 5)
```

To help you get some practice in writing out the classes that you want to use, take a few minutes to open up your compiler and type this in. As you can see with this example, there are a lot of parts that we need to look through. First, you see that there is a definition for the object. And then you see the attributes and the method definition.

IN addition to the above, there is going to be the class definition, the part of the code known as the destructor function, and then finally we are to the function. This is a lot of parts to keep track of, and it likely that you may not understand what is going on with each part, so let's break them all up and explore how they work and why they are so important to create your class in Python.

First, we have the object instantiation and class definition. These are both when it comes to the syntax of creating your class. This is because they are going to tell the code what needs to happen to get things done. The class definition is going to be the part of the code that we did above that says "`class subclass(superclass0)`", and then the part that comes with object instantiation is going to be the part that says "`object = class()`."

Then some special attributes come with this code. There are a few different special attributes that you can add to your code, depending on what you want to get done. Being able to understand what these attributes are all about will ensure that you can create a code the way that you want, and it also ensures that the interpreter knows what needs to happen in this part of the program. There are some special attributes that you can work within your code, but some of the most important ones—and the ones that you are going to use the most often as a beginner in Python include:

`__dict__`   this is the direct variable of a class namespace

`__doc__`   this is the document reference string of class

`__name__`   this will be the class name

`__module__`this is the module name and consists of the class

`__bases__`   this is the tuple that will also contain all of the superclasses

Memorizing these can help you out, but it may be nice to learn how they work inside of the code. Here is an example below that you can try out by typing into your compiler.

```
class Cat(object):
        itsWeight = 0
        itsAge = 0
        itsName = ""
        defMeow(self):
        print("Meow!")


        defDisplayCat(self):
        print("I   am   a   Cat   Object,   My   name   is",
self.itsName)
        print("My age is", self.itsAge)
        print("My weight is", self.itsWeight)

frisky = Cat()
frisky.itsAge = 10
frisky.itsName = "Frisky"
frisky.DisplayCat()
frisky.Meow()
```

When you are using this as your syntax in the interpreter, the result that you will get on the screen is:

```
('I am a Cat Object, My name is,' 'Frisky')
```

```
('My age is,' 10)
('My weight is,' 0)
Meow!
```

Once we are done with this part of the code, we are going to move onto the idea of accessing different members of your class. When you look through some of the different examples that we have done in this chapter, you may notice that we spent some time trying to identify our object, which, in this case, is `cat`, as being called Frisky. We were able to do that with the help of the dot operator.

This was helpful because it ensured that our program was able to access the members of the objects correctly. If you then look back at some of the code that we did before, you will notice that there are a fair number of variables that we can find inside of it. Sometimes, all of these variables may not make sense to use, especially since they are often inconvenient, and they are going to make a mess of the code that you are working with.

But there are times when you do need to have all of these variables present. How are you supposed to handle this and still make sure the code is going to work properly? You can use a few options to help you deal with this, without all of the issues. We are going to focus on the method that many programmers like to work with because it is easier to use. And this method is known as the accessor information. This is a good option because it helps you to get the information that you need without as much work.

You will find that it is straightforward to work with this method to help you take care of all those variables without a big mess. The syntax that works the best for ensuring that this can happen will include:

```
class Cat(object)
      itsAge = None
      itsWeight = None
      itsName = None
      #set accessor function use to assign values to
the fields or member vars
      def setItsAge(self, itsAge):
      self.itsAge = itsAge

      def setItsWeight(self, itsWeight):
      self.itsWeight = itsWeight

      def setItsName(self, itsName):
      self.itsName =itsName

      #get accessor function use to return the values
from a field
      def getItsAge(self):
      return self.itsAge
      def getItsWeight(self):
      return self.itsWeight
```

```
        def getItsName(self):
        return self.itsName

objFrisky = Cat()
objFrisky.setItsAge(5)
objFrisky.setItsWeight(10)
objFrisky.setItsName("Frisky")
print("Cats Name is:", objFrisky.getItsname())
print("Its age is:", objFrisky.getItsAge())
print("Its weight is:", objFrisky.getItsName())
```

The output that you are going to get from all of this will be the following:

```
('Cats Name is:', 'Frisky')
(Its age is:', 5)
('Its weight is:,' 10)
```

With the method that we just worked with above, we were able to place that accessor method and then we took a few steps to check whether or not it was able to work with the variables that we chose. This is going to be a good thing to work with because it helps us later during a few processes in Python, including data hiding and data encapsulation. When you want to make sure that the members who use the program can access the information, you will need to make sure that this method is open up to the public or some people will be blocked on it. But you also have the option of turning the viewing into either private or protected based on your own needs.

It is so important to know a bit about how the objects and classes in Python are going to work for you. If you can use them properly, these will not be all that complicated, but they will ensure that there is the right kind of organization of all the information in the code, ensuring that the program is going to run the way that you want. Take some time to practice a few of the codes that we have in this chapter to help you learn better how these classes work, and how you can use them on your projects.

Chapter 11: What Are the Operators and How Do You Use Them?

The next topic that we are going to explore in our Python codes are the operators. We have talked about these a bit throughout this guidebook, but now, we need to take a closer look at the way that they work, as well as why they can be so important to your success with writing. The good news is that these are pretty simple to work with, and it is likely that if you have done any coding so far, you have used a few of these operators already. However, since they can do some pretty amazing things with your code, it is worth our time to take a look at how to use them and all of the different things that they can do. Hence, with that introduction, let's take a closer look at how some of the operators are going to work when you are using Python.

Working with the Arithmetic Operator

The first type of operator that you will be able to use with your Python codes, and can be used regularly is the arithmetic operator. If you need to add together a few parts of your code, or you need to do some math inside of the code, then these operators are going to be the best ones for you to use. Whether you need to add, multiply, divide, or subtract, you will be able to use these operators to help you get the work done. The arithmetic operators that you are likely to use in Python include

(+): This sign is the operator for addition. Any time that you need to add together two parts of the code, you will use this operator.

(-): This is the sign for the operator of subtraction. Any time that you need to subtract two parts of your code, you are going to use this operator.

(*): This sign is the operator for multiplication. Any time that you would like to multiply together the two parts of a particular code, you would use this operator.

(/): This sign is the operator for dividing. Any time that you would like to divide two parts of the code, you can work with this operator.

When you are working in the Python language, you will be able to use any of these operators at any time that it is needed. You can even use more than one of these operators at the same time if it is needed. If you do bring in more than one type of the arithmetic operators in the same part of the code, you have to remember the order of operations. This means that you will handle the multiplier operators first, and then you go to the division, making sure you go from the left side to the right side. Once those are done, you can do all of the addition operators and end with the subtraction operators, going from left to right as well.

Working with the Comparison Operators

In addition to using the arithmetic operators, you can also work inside your code with the comparison operator. These comparison operators are a great option to work with any time that you have two or more values or statements that show up in the code, and you are looking to compare them or bring them together.

It is common to see these when you are working with Boolean expressions because they need to work from the idea of the statements, either being the same or being different, which is true or false. You will either have it that the statements or the numbers you are working within the code end up being the same, or they are not the same. This is how we come to working with the Boolean expressions. Some of the different operators that fit in this category in the Python language include:

(>=): this one means to check if the left-hand operand is greater than or equal to the value of the one on the right.

(<=) : this one means to check if the value of the left-hand operand is less than or equal to the one on the right.

(>) : this one means to check whether the values of the left side are greater than the value on the right side of the code.

(<) : this one means to check whether the values of the left side are less than the values that are on the right side.

(!=) : this is the "not equal to" operator.

(==) : this one is the "equal to" operator.

As you go through this and work on the program or the code, you may find that you have already started to use this kind of operator in some of the codes that we already have, and you haven't even realized it yet! You can easily set up some conditions inside of the code, and when you do this, you want to make sure that the code will meet these conditions before it continues. This is where the comparison operators are going to come in and be helpful.

With this idea, you will have your comparison in place, and then the user can come on and put in the information they want. The comparison operator is then going to take a look at that input, and compare it against the conditions that you set. This allows the program to figure out if the input and the condition you set are the same or different from each other. This can help you get more out of the program and ensures that you get the right results with your program.

Working with the Logical Operators

The third type of operators that you can work within Python will be the logical operators. These are a good kind of operator to work with because they can take the input that the user gives to them, and then evaluate that information based on the conditions that the programmer put into that code. There are a few types of operators that are going to fit into this idea, but the three common ones, and the ones that a beginner is most likely to use for their programs, will include:

Or: This is the logical operator that will have the compiler is going to value "x," and if it is false, then it is going to move on and evaluate y. If it notices that x is true, then the compiler is going to return the evaluation of x to the user.

And: With this one, if x is the false answer, then the compiler will stop and evaluate that statement or that part of the code. But if x ends up being the true part, it will skip that part of the code, and move on to evaluating y.

Not: If the compiler looks at x and finds that it is false, then the compiler is going to return the result of True. On the other hand, if x is true, then the program is going to return False as the answer.

As you can see, these logical operators are pretty similar to what we saw with the comparison operators. But you will find that these kinds of operators are going to work a bit differently. You will only need to work with these types of operators when you need to use the specific situations that we listed above, and not for every situation.

Working with the Assignment Operators

The final operator type that you can work within Python is the assignment operator. This one is going to use the equal sign to take one or more values (usually it is one with beginner programming, but can easily be more if you choose), over to any variable that you are working with. So, if you would like to take your chosen variable and assign 100 to it as the value, you will need to put an equal sign between the two of these to show that the value is assigned to that variable in the code.

There are going to be some times when you will write out a particular code and will need to use the assignment operator, using it in the code so that it knows what value is assigned to the variable. If you look through some of the different codes that we have worked on throughout this guidebook, there are various examples of how the assignment operator can use. Any time that you would like to talk with the compiler and have it assign a value to the variable, then this assignment operator is what you need to use so that the compiler knows what value is there.

As we briefly mentioned, it is possible to take more than one value and assign it to the variable that you would use. Doing this is easier than it may seem, as long as you make sure to list it all out in the proper manner to get this to work for you. You need to have the right signs in place and make sure that you put the equal sign in between the values that are meant to go with that chosen variable. You don't have to limit yourself to just two or three values to the variable if you want to expand this out more. It is possible to assign as many values to the same variable if you would like.

Of course, the more values that you try to assign to the same variable, the more complicated the code is going to get. As a beginner, it is often best to stick with the codes that will just put one or two values to each variable, and then work up to some of the more complicated things as you go. This is going to make the process of writing out code a lot easier, and you won't have to worry about where the signs go and whether or not the compiler is going to understand what you are doing.

Because this is a very common operator to work with and it has a lot of power behind it, it is important that you learn how to use this kind of operator. There are a lot of times when you are going to have a variable in your code, and it is going to be useless if you don't assign some value to it. This value is going to make sure that the compiler can call up the variable, and that it is going to be usable in the code that you are writing. But if you don't know how to work with the assignment operator, then putting value back to the variable is going to become impossible.

As you can see, these operators, in all of their different forms, are going to be important parts of the code that you are working on. The ones that we have gone through above for this chapter are some of the most common operators that you can work with, and they are going to make it easier for you to do some neat things in your code.

You can use these operators to add in some more power, to compare some of the information that you want to use in your code, and adding them will be easy. You just need to look through the different types of code that we have gone through in this guidebook, and all of the examples and even though they are seen as basic codes to help you get more familiar with this coding language, they are still going to contain a lot of the different operators that we just talked about. No matter what kind of code you decide to work with, you are going to find a lot of use when you learn how to work with these operators.

Chapter 12: The Variables in the Python Language

We have spent a lot of different topics inside this guidebook so far. We have looked at how to work with inheritances, how to make our exceptions inside a code, how to create our loops, and so much more. Now, we need to take a look at the next topic of variables and how they are going to work in the Python code.

To keep this process simple, the variables are going to be anything inside the code that can hold onto a value that may or may not change. The variable is just like a box that can hold onto things, mainly information in this case. And they are essential for a programmer to work with, in Python and other coding languages, because these variables will ensure that when the code runs, the compiler is going to be able to pull out the right value at the right time.

These variables are just going to be like a stored into the memory of your computer and in the code. You will then be able to tell the compiler that you want these variables to be pulled out when it is time. This means that the variables that you go and write into the code are stored and found on a specific location in the memory of your computer. If they were not stored in that specific point, then it would be hard for the compiler to bring these back up when you were running the code.

You want to make sure that the variables are given the right value as you work through this kind of code. It makes it easier for you to pull up the values that are assigned to it at a later point. Depending on the data you want to put into the code, the variable can save the right space in the memory of your computer and makes it easier to find it later on.

How Do I Assign a Value Over to the Variable?

Before the variable can do the job that it needs to, it has to have at least one value that is assigned to it. Otherwise, it is just an empty box found on the memory of the computer, with nothing in it. It isn't going to pull up anything on the computer when the program decides to go through and run the program. If the variable as a value assigned to it the way that it should (and at times, you will want to have more than one value assigned back to the same variable), then it is more likely to react the way you are looking for with your code as long as you did everything else right in the code.

As you get more familiar with working on these variables, you will find that these come in three different options that you can use. Each of them is going to be brought up in different situations based on the code that you want to write, and the type of value that you decide to assign to that variable. Some of the main choices that you will get to work with when it comes to variable types include:

Float: this would include numbers like 3.14 and so on.
String: this is going to be like a statement where you could write out something like "Thank you for visiting my page!" or another similar phrase.
Whole number: this would be any of the other numbers that you would use that do not have a decimal point.

When you decide to work with some variables in your code, you must remember that you won't have to take the time to make any declarations before a spot in the memory is saved for you. This is something that automatically happens once you use the equal sign and get the value assigned over to the variable as we talked about in the operators. If you want to double check and see if this is what is going to happen when you run the code, look to see if there is an equal sign that appears before the value or values and the variable that they are assigned to.

The process of assigning a value or values over to your chosen variable is going to be a simple process to work with. You need to work with the equal sign between the two of these to make it work. A couple of good examples of how you can do this will include:

```
x = 12              #this  is  an  example  of  an  integer
assignment
pi = 3.14   #this  is  an  example  of  a  floating  point
assignment
customer name = John Doe      #this  is  an  example  of  a
string assignment
```

Another option that you can do here, and that we have mentioned a little bit in this chapter already is to have a variable assigned to two or more values. There are some instances when you are writing code, and you will need to take two values and place them with the same variable.

To do this, you need to use the same procedure that we talked about above. Just make sure that you add in an equal sign to each part to help the compiler know that these are all associated with the same variable. So, you would want to write out something like `a = b = c = 1` to show the compiler that each of these variables equals one. Or you could have `1 = b = 2` to show that there are two values to a variable.

The most important thing to remember here is that the variable needs to be assigned to a value to work in the code and that these variables are simply spots that are reserved in the memory for those values. Then, when the compiler needs to call up those values, it simply will call up the variable to bring everything out.

As you can see, working with variables can be a simple process, but it is still something that you should spend some time with. There are a lot of different things that you can save in a variable, and assigning the right value or values over to your variable will ensure that the compiler can bring them up and provides you with the results that you need. Make sure to practice assigning a value over to the variable of your choice, and even assigning multiple values over to the variable of your choice so that you can get more familiar with how all of this works.

Chapter 13: Troubleshooting a Python Program When Things Aren't Working as Planned

As a beginner, the idea of writing out a whole coding language can sometimes seem like a big deal and something overwhelming to work with. We took a lot of time to look at the different parts of the code that you can work with and explored some examples to help you see what works and what might not work in your code.

As you are starting to learn more about Python coding and all of the different parts that come with it, you may run into some troubles that you are going to need to deal with. Maybe your program isn't working the way that you think it should, and you keep getting an error message that shouldn't be there—or perhaps you don't know how to fix the problem when you do run into this issue. The good news is there are some simple things that even a beginner can do with their program to get it up and running and to ensure that they are going to be able to get back to coding sooner. Some of the best troubleshooting ideas that you can work within Python include:

Print Out the Code Often

It is never a good idea to write out hours of code, and then go and test it. This may work if you get everything right. But if you get something wrong, you now need to go back through and fix all of the things that you did wrong. And that is a lot of code to go through and look for errors. Printing the information out and testing the code regularly will ensure that you aren't going to run into this problem.

This doesn't mean that you have to print out after each line. But it does mean to print often. If you can print out after each small bit of code, this will make it easier when things aren't working the way that you want. If you have been printing out the information after every five minutes of coding for example, and all of a sudden something in the code isn't working, you know exactly where the mistake is, and you won't have to go through and search through all of the pages and all of the coding again.

Start with Some of the Codes You Already Know

As a beginner, there is a lot of new stuff that you are going to need to focus on to ensure that you get the results that you want out of your project. But thanks to the information in this guidebook, you now know how to work on some of the basics of the code in Python. When you are in doubt about some of the things that you need to do in different situations, then it is a good idea to do some practice with existing code, and codes that you know work already.

Many beginners find that it is better for them to start with some structures and syntaxes that are in existence already, and then you can go through and make the small changes that are needed for your code. This ensures that the code is going to work, and can save some headaches along the way. As you use these existing code structures and learn how they work a bit more, you will then be able to write them on your own. But in the beginning, this is a good way to get started and see the results that you want.

When you are ready to work on a project on your own, then there are a lot of resources that you can use to help you find the code that you want to work with. A quick Google search is going to be able to help you find the structure of the code that you need. It doesn't have to be what you will need for that project exactly, but having the basic syntax is going to make things easier and will help you to get the code started. From there, you can make the changes that you want and then check out the code to make sure that all of the implanted changes are the ones that you want.

After Small Changes, Run the Code to Check It Out

Do not start with a blank file, sit down, and spend an hour coding before you even try out the code for the first time. You will make the work harder for yourself, and when there are a whole bunch of little errors that pop up, you won't know where to start. It can take forever to go through it all and fix whatever is going wrong.

Instead, every few minutes, you should run the updates and test the code to see if something comes up. That way, when a bug does show up in the code, you only have a few lines or so of the code to check for the issue rather than a whole bunch of code. It isn't possible for you to test out your code too often, so do it as much as you can.

Always remember that the more code that you write before you test it again, the more places where errors can occur and the more code that you will need to search through again. And each time that you do go through and run the code, you will get some more feedback on your work so you can learn as you go.

This may seem like it is slowing down your coding skills and what you can do to get the code done, but in reality, it is going to make a difference for what you can get done, and the amount of time that you will spend on each project. If you have to go through and have to change the information on two hours of work, then this is going to take longer to find the mistake than it is worth. If you have to go through and heck a small block of code at a time, then you will be able to find the error faster and get back on to your coding.

Take the Time to Read Any Error Messages

If you do make a mistake in some of the codes that you are writing, you are going to see an error message show up. When this does happen, you should read through the description, because this can point out what is wrong with your code and how you can fix it. Let's say that you get an error message that says that the language runtime tried to execute the program but ran into a problem. What this means is that you skipped on a step in your code writing, or there was a typo, or something else is missing from the code. You will know what to fix from this information and can get int here and make sure it is done.

If you are first getting started with Python programming, then it is possible that a message will come up and you won't understand what it is saying. But you should still read through it and see what information is there. At a minimum, you will at least get a line number on this message, and you can take a look on that line of your code to see what is going on.

For those who have tried the other steps and still are not able to figure out what the error message is all about, then you do have the option of going online and searching for it. Some error messages can be confusing, and even if you go back through the lines and try to check, you may not be able to find the error and how to fix it.

Doing an online search can help tell you exactly what is going on. You can copy and paste the last line of that error message into Google and see what comes up. There will likely be at least a few results when you type this in as other coders were probably met with this message and had questions as well. This should provide you with some information on what is wrong in the code, and you can go back through and figure out what is wrong with your code and fix it all up.

Even though this is a great way to get answers to the questions that you have, especially when you are not able to figure out what the error message means—but don't just run to this for every time that an error message shows up. You aren't going to learn much about coding and how to fix your own mistakes if you are just relying on Google to answer all of your questions.

Try to take a look at the error and look through the code to see if you can fix it on your own. And then, if you get stuck, utilize this option for your own needs.

Guess on the Fix and Then Check It Out

If you try a few of the other methods and still aren't sure about how to fix something, you may need to try out a few different things to see what is going to happen. You should already be running your code as often as possible to provide you with some quick feedback. Keep doing this as you try out a few options and see whether it fixes your error or not.

There is a possibility that the fix you are trying is going to introduce a new error, and sometimes it can be hard to tell if you are nearing a solution or making things worse. Try not to do this for so long that you have no idea how to get back to your starting position.

Trying out a few different things can be important because it helps you to learn more about your code and then if you do ask someone else for help, they are going to ask you what you have tried already. They probably will be more annoyed than anything if they hear that you haven't tried anything, but if you list out a few things that you already tried, then they know where to start from that place.

Use the Process of Commenting Out the Code

No matter what kind of coding language you decide to work with, there is going to be the option to comment in your work. This is a way that you can leave a little note or some information in the code, but in a way that ensures that the compiler isn't going to try and execute that note in the program. This can be an advantage for you as you write the code because you will also be able to use it to help troubleshoot the issues in your project.

If you are writing some code and find that you keep getting an error message, but nothing that you are doing seems to work to fix it, then you may want to comment out the code. You can pick a part of the code that you think is causing the issue, and then just at the # sign to the front of it. This takes it out of the code basically, without erasing all of it.

If the script that you are working on is pretty long, then you can go through here and comment out some of the parts of the code, specifically the parts that aren't going to have a direct relation to the changes that you plan to work on. This is going to help because you will be able to search through just the code that has the mistake, and it speeds up the whole process.

Be careful when you are doing the commenting out process; you do need to be a bit careful. It isn't going to help you too much if you end up commenting out the parts that are needed to set the variables. If you do this, then the program is going to stop working, and you will end up with a mess trying to get the program to run. Start by commenting out just small parts of the code first and add on as you need to do more testing. It ensures that you don't eliminate some parts of the code that you need at that time.

After you have finished using the "commenting out" method to help you test your code, and you are sure that it is ready to go without the error, then it is time to go back through the code and remove any comment characters that you put there. This takes some time, but it will help you to turn the whole program on so that it runs the application that you were writing.

Ask Someone for Help If It Is Needed

At some point, you may have tried the troubleshooting options that we have listed above, and maybe even a few others of your own, and you are still not able to get the code to behave in the manner that you would like. If you have done all of that and still see an error message that you are not able to fix yet, then it is time to see if there is someone else out there who you can ask for help.

Every programmer needs help at some point or another, and there is nothing wrong with asking and receiving help when you get stuck. If you do ask for help (hopefully after taking a small break from doing the coding to ensure that you are not overworking yourself and missing some big things that you could fix), you need to have the following things in place and ready to answer so that the other person knows how to help you out exactly:

Explain what you want the program to do for you and where the error is occurring.
Show the other person the code that is sending you an error so they can see it for themselves.
Show the other person the stack trace, all of it, including the message you got stating the error.
Explain everything that you have already tried on the error. This helps the other person have a good idea of what you have tried, and what they should try to get the code to work.

Working on a Python code can be a rewarding experience. There are a lot of benefits to working with this code—and as you can see from the examples in this guidebook, as well as some of the troubleshooting that we just looked at, there are also a lot of neat codes and other programs that you can write, even as a beginner!

Conclusion

Thank you for making it through to the end of *Python Programming*! Let's hope it was informative and able to provide you with all of the tools you need to achieve your goals—whatever they may be.

The next step is to get started with writing some of your codes using the great Python coding language to help you out. This guidebook gave you all of the tools that you need to get started with this kind of language. We explored what the Python language is all about, along with many of the benefits that seem to draw programmers in, whether they are beginners or not, and entices them to get started with this language. We even looked at the steps that you need to take to start installing this program on your computer, no matter what kind of operating system you are using.

Writing a new coding language can sometimes seem complicated. You may worry that the text and all of the little parts of it are going to be too complicated for you to figure out on your own—and this is what keeps a lot of people away from trying out this code, in the first place. However, when it comes to working with a particular code in this language, all of those fears can be put to rest. As you saw throughout this guidebook and the many codes that we explored, writing out a particular code in this language is easy and fun to do! Even as a beginner, you are going to catch on quickly.

This guidebook is full of all the different codes, syntaxes, and information that you need to get started with writing some of your codes. We not only took a look at how to install this program on your computer—but we also broke down how to work with many of the common things that show up in this language. Whether your coding will require you to work with exceptions, loops, conditional statements, regular expressions, inheritances, or a combination of them all (and some of the other topics that we discussed in this guidebook), you now know exactly how to use them to your advantage when you write out some of your codes.

There are so many benefits that can come from working on a Python code for your reasons. Beginners love this language for so many reasons—and now that you know a bit more about it and how all of the different parts of the code work together, you can easily see why they are even more advanced coders are drawn to this language for some of their projects. It is incredible how something easy to use can be so powerful, and have so much diversity and options to go with it. When you are ready to learn more about the Python coding language and try out some of the different codes that we talked about, then make sure to check out this guidebook, and use it to get started!